CARMACK OF THE KLONDIKE

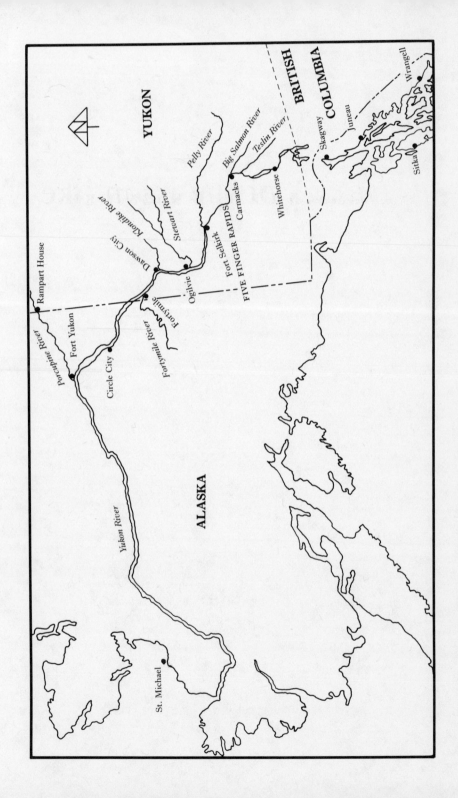

Carmack of the Klondike

by

James Albert Johnson

Epicenter Press and Horsdal & Schubart

This book is co-published by

Epicenter Press   Horsdal & Schubart Publishers Ltd.
18821 64th Avenue NE   and   Box 1
Seattle, WA, USA   Ganges, BC, Canada, V0S 1E0
98155

   or

Box 60529
Fairbanks, AK, USA
99706

Background cover photograph by Mike Gluss, Ganges, BC.
Portraits on the front cover courtesy of Ernest C. Saftig and Northwest Collections, University of Washington, Seattle.
Chapter-head drawings by Tim Williamson, Ganges, BC.
Maps drawn by Jim Smith, Island Drafting, Ganges, BC.
Design and typesetting by The Typeworks, Vancouver, BC.
This book is set in Imprint. Printed and bound in the United States.

Canadian Cataloguing in Publication Data
Johnson, James Albert, 1905-
    Carmack of the Klondike
    Includes bibliographical references.
    ISBN 0-920663-10-9
    1. Carmack, George W. (George Washington).
2. Yukon Territory--Biography. 3. Klondike
River Valley (Yukon)--Gold discoveries.
I. Title.
FC4022.1.C37J64   1990   971.9'102'092
F1093.C37J64   1990   C90-091457-2

Library of Congress Cataloging-in-Publication Data
Johnson, James Albert, 1905-
    Carmack of the Klondike / James Albert Johnson.
        p.   cm.
    Includes bibliographical references and index.
    ISBN 0-945397-08-9 (pbk.) : $14.95
    1. Carmack, George W. (George Washington). 1860–1922. 2. Klondike
River Valley (Yukon)--Gold discoveries. 3. Pioneers--Yukon--
Klondike River Valley--Biography. I. Title.
F1095.K5J64   1990
971.9'4--dc20
[B]   90-3820
                                                                 CIP

Contents

v

Introduction and Acknowledgements

I'll never forget the day I learned of the Carmack letters. It was the day I fell off a ladder.

On an August morning in 1957, I was standing on a ladder in the Alaska section of the Shorey Book Store in Seattle, trying to read titles on the top shelf. Suddenly, an unseen hand grabbed one of my trouser cuffs and gave it a couple of yanks, as a conductor might pull the bell-cord on a San Francisco cable car. I looked down and saw a middle-aged man smiling up at me.

"You interested in books on Alaska?" he asked.

Annoyed, I was tempted to ask this fellow sarcastically what he thought I was doing five feet off the floor in a section of Alaska books. Instead, I simply nodded.

"Well," he said, "I have some books for sale that came from Judge Wickersham's library. They have his bookplates. Interested?"

I certainly was. Wickersham had been one of Alaska's first federal judges and later served as a territorial delegate to Congress. In my excitement as I climbed down, my foot missed a rung and I found myself sitting on the floor.

The stranger introduced himself as Herbert Beatty and took me to his home on Queen Anne Hill. He explained on the way that he had bought two boxes of books bearing the Wickersham bookplate for $20 from a second-hand store. When Wickersham died in 1938, most of his collection of 18,000 Alaska volumes was sold to the Alaska Territorial

Library in Juneau. The judge had hundreds of duplicate titles, which had been sold to book-dealers in Seattle and New York City.

I bought 24 Wickersham books from Beatty and as I bent over to pick them up, I stumbled over an apple crate filled with old letters and personal papers.

"Whose letters?" I asked.

"G.W. Carmack. Ever heard of him?"

My eyes widened and my mouth flew open. "GEORGE CARMACK!? The man whose Bonanza Creek discovery started the Klondike Gold Rush!?"

For the second time that day, I found myself sitting on the floor, this time reading a letter dated June 20, 1897, written by George Carmack to his sister, Rose Watson, and her husband. Carmack told them of the richness of his gold claims and invited them to join him on Bonanza Creek, offering detailed directions on how to get there and what to bring. His diary was in the box too, as were bank books, legal documents and family photographs.

I bought the Carmack papers for $500. They were to disclose a wealth of new details about the Klondike gold rush, and the role Carmack played in starting it. Over a period of 40 years, Carmack had written regularly to his sister in California. She saved more than a hundred letters, which told of Carmack's life before and after he found fame in the Yukon. They inspired me to conduct additional research, and I set out to trace the circuitous route taken by the letters before they came into my hands. This is what I discovered:

After Carmack died in 1922, his sister and daughter fought a four-year legal battle with Carmack's widow over the Carmack estate. Rose sent the letters to her Seattle attorney for use as evidence. The squabbling relatives reached an out-of-court settlement, however, and for the next dozen years the letters gathered dust in the attorney's office.

When James Wickersham came to Seattle seeking medical treatment for his failing eyesight in 1938, he persuaded the attorney to hand over not only the Carmack correspondence but also a thick file of legal documents. Wickersham took the papers back to Juneau, where they remained until his death a year later.

What happened then is unclear. However, by the early 1950s, the Carmack letters had been returned to Seattle among the personal effects of an unidentified guest staying at the William Penn Hotel, whose belongings were seized for failure to pay his bill.

In 1957, the hotel cleaned out a basement storage room and donated ten boxes of unclaimed property to St. Vincent de Paul, the Catholic charity. Beatty purchased the Wickersham books from the charity's second-hand store and saved the Carmack letters from certain destruction.

And that's how I came into possession of the Carmack letters, which form the foundation for this work. All the facts in this book are based on material in the Carmack papers; in some instances, I have created dialogue that seemed appropriate, to bring the story alive.

I am grateful to those who helped me with additional research. I owe a debt of gratitude to Carmack's daughter, Graphie Grace Carmack Rogers. My special thanks go to her son, Ernest Charles Saftig, who graciously loaned me his treasured family photographs. I was fortunate to interview Patsy Henderson of Carcross, himself an important Klondike figure. My hearty thanks to Aubrey Simmons of Carcross for his vivid recollections of Kate Carmack and her relatives. Bill Mathews and Mrs. Fred Boss of Skagway knew Skookum Jim and shared their memories with me. Former Klondiker Ed Conrad contributed Carmack anecdotes, as did Lavina Elliot and Paul McKenna.

I am grateful to Mrs. W.W. (Carol) Bell of Seattle, a distant cousin of Carmack, who furnished important dates of births, marriages and deaths gleaned from her mother's Bible. I also wish to thank Mrs. Arthur H. Howard, Morris C. Jung and Frank Brink for their assistance.

For their courtesy and help, I am grateful to staff members of the Yukon Archives, Whitehorse; the National Archives, Washington, D.C.; the Alaska Historical Library, Juneau; the Museum of History and Industry, Seattle; the University of Washington Library; the Klondike Gold Rush National Historical Park; the Seattle Public Library, the Martinez (Calif.) Public Library, and the Vancouver (B.C.) Public Library.

Ann Saling reviewed several early versions of my manuscript and I am indebted to her for many valuable suggestions.

Finally, I thank Lael Morgan, Sue Mattson and Kent Sturgis of Epicenter Press, and Marlyn Horsdal of Horsdal & Schubart Publishers Ltd. for their unceasing encouragement and editing skill in preparing the final manuscript for publication.

James Albert Johnson

Chapter 1

Klondike Miners
Strike Golden Paystreak

At the entrance to Bill McPhee's saloon in the Yukon River mining camp of Fortymile, George Carmack kicked the mud and sand of the Yukon from his boots, pushed open the door and walked in. As he scanned the crowd of miners clustered around the bar and the poker tables, he pulled on the drooping ends of the bushy brown mustache that almost encircled his chin. The pale blue air reeked of stale tobacco smoke and unwashed bodies. Sounds from a dozen raucous conversations rippled across the saloon, almost as loud as the roar of a swollen mountain stream. As he sauntered up to the bar on that August evening in 1896, Carmack displayed no outward evidence of his inner excitement.

He shook hands with bartender Clarence Berry, then ordered a whiskey, his first drink in almost a year. Tonight, he felt he had good reason to celebrate, so he ordered another drink. Grinning and glowing after his second whiskey, Carmack turned to face the crowd. Raising his hand and his voice, he called for quiet. His widely spaced blue eyes revealed his excitement but his voice was calm.

"Boys, I've got some good news. There's been a big strike up the river."

"A strike!" shouted a brawny poker player. "That ain't no news. That's just a scheme of Ladue and Harper to start a stampede up by their trading post."

"There's where you're off, my friend," Carmack replied amiably. "Neither Ladue nor Harper knows anything about this."

Carmack picked up a small brass pan near the gold scales at the end of the bar. He pulled a cartridge shell out of his pocket, unplugged it, and emptied out its contents. Flaky gold nuggets lay in the pan.

"Well, how does that look to you, eh?"

"Is that some of the Miller Creek gold that Ladue gave you?" asked the burly loudmouth as he left the poker table and swaggered up to the bar. Picking up the blower pan, he spread the gold around with his forefinger, blew away a few particles of black sand, and then carefully inspected the tiny gold nuggets.

"Boys, this ain't no Miller Creek gold. I know the gold from every creek in this country and this ain't like none of them. It looks different and feels different. Say, old man, if it ain't asking too much, where in hell did you find this gold?"

"Well, I don't think it was anywhere near that place, but gather 'round and I'll tell you where I did find it."

The room noise subsided as Carmack told how he had discovered coarse gold and nuggets in the Klondike area on a small stream known as Rabbit Creek. He had renamed it Bonanza Creek, he said. He had staked his Discovery Claim about 15 miles up from the mouth of the creek, which flows into the Klondike River less than a mile above its junction with the Yukon.[1]

Some of the old-timers in the crowd were skeptical of Carmack's story. Several years ago a rumor had spread up and down the Yukon River mining camps that the Klondike side of the Yukon was barren of gold. Some miners who had unsuccessfully prospected the Klondike area referred to it as a moose pasture. But the few small nuggets that Carmack produced were convincing evidence. There was gold in the Klondike country, some 55 miles upriver from Fortymile—not just fine flour gold, but coarse gold.

After Carmack finished telling his story, the excited crowd began to thin as one man after another hurried out the door to find a partner, rustle up a boat, and get outfitted for the journey upriver to the Klondike.

The fastest way to get from Fortymile to the Klondike was by poling boat. The day after Carmack made his announcement, every boat in Fortymile disappeared as miners abandoned their claims in the local diggings and stampeded upriver.

Bartender Clarence Berry was one of the first to leave. Grubstaked by Bill McPhee, Berry obtained a boat and a supply of provisions from the Alaska Commercial Company store. With another stampeder to help him propel the boat, Berry started up the Yukon. Each man carrying a long pole, they walked from bow to stern of the boat, taking turns poling it upstream.

After an exhausting two-day journey, Berry and his friend reached the mouth of the Klondike, where they cached their boat. Without stopping to rest, the two men hiked up the Bonanza valley in search of Carmack's Discovery Claim. They were not alone. Dozens of prospectors were already on the creek and had staked claims. Berry arrived in time to stake No. 42 Above Discovery on Bonanza.

During the long, cold winter of 1896–97, Carmack and his lucky neighbors doggedly worked their claims. Though the placer claims were probably the richest ever staked on the North American continent, that winter the outside world knew nothing of the great outpouring of wealth.

In mid-June of 1897, the first riverboat of the season, the *Alice,* owned by the Alaska Commercial Company, churned up the ice-free Yukon. The sternwheeler brought much-needed supplies of food to Dawson City, the booming mining camp of 50 log cabins and 500 tents that had sprung up on the swampy flats at the mouth of the Klondike.

Although Dawson City and the Klondike mining district were situated on Canadian soil and governed by Canadian laws, most of the men working in the area were American citizens. The saloons of Dawson City were crowded with boisterous miners, their pockets heavy with gold, celebrating the arrival of the *Alice* by drinking real whiskey. Two days later, the *Portus B. Weare,* a steamer operated by the rival North American Transportation and Trading Company, tied up at Dawson City. Saloon keepers continued to reap a rich harvest of gold.

Silver coins and paper money, known as "cheechako money," were scarce in Dawson City. The universal medium of exchange was gold dust, measured in Troy ounces. One ounce of gold was worth $17. In the saloons, a pinch of gold dust passed for a dollar. Bartenders earned an ounce and a half for a day's work, more if they were endowed with unusually large thumbs.

What to do with their gold—after buying all the food, drinks and supplies they could use—became a problem for the miners. Dawson City had no bank where surplus gold could be converted to greenbacks or certificates of deposit. Many a miner dumped his gold dust and nuggets into empty tobacco or syrup cans and then stashed the cans in his cabin. Dozens of men entrusted their heavy pokes of gold to saloon keepers, who tossed them under the bar for safekeeping.

More than 80 miners, loaded with gold, booked passage on the *Alice* and the *Weare* for the 1,650-mile trip down the Yukon to the Bering Sea port of St. Michael, where they would transfer to ocean steamers. They had come into the Yukon country the hard way, laboriously packing their prospecting outfits over the rugged Chilkoot Pass trail. Now they were leaving the Yukon as rich men, traveling the easy way, as fare-paying passengers on the two riverboats. Some of the departing miners had sold out and were leaving the Klondike forever, to enjoy the comforts and luxuries made possible by their new wealth. Others were simply going outside for a rest, leaving behind partners who would continue working their claims.

George Carmack, not yet rich, remained in the Klondike and kept on digging for gold.

Clarence Berry, the former bartender, became one of the wealthiest men in the Klondike after he traded a half-interest in his No. 42 Above Discovery on Bonanza for a half-interest in No. 6 on Eldorado Creek nearby. In addition, Berry and his partner had purchased No. 4 and No. 5 on Eldorado. After Berry had washed out his winter dumps and paid off his workmen, he had $130,000 in gold for his winter's work. When Berry and his wife boarded the *Alice,* friends helped them lug aboard a sagging suitcase and two stout wooden boxes stuffed with gold.

Other miners packed loads of gold aboard the ships in a strange assortment of containers—bulging gold belts, whiskey bottles, homemade pokes of canvas or moosehide, even tied up in blanket rolls slung over their shoulders.

Thomas S. Lippy, formerly the general secretary for the Y.M.C.A. in Seattle, was another neophyte prospector who took a chance. Accompanied by his wife and young son, Lippy had arrived in the Klondike too late to stake on Bonanza, so he staked on Eldorado. When Lippy boarded the *Alice* he had $65,000 in gold with him. Left behind in his winter dump, for his partners to wash out, was still more gold, estimated to be worth $150,000.

William Stanley, formerly a Seattle bookseller, was another argonaut who found the golden fleece. After washing out $112,000 in gold, he threw down his shovel and shouted, "Goodbye, old boy! I'll never pick you up again."[2]

The rest of the Klondike miners on the *Alice* and the *Weare* were carrying various amounts of gold worth from $5,000 to $50,000—all this at a time when millions of American working men were earning less than $50 a month and a man could provide a comfortable living for his family on the interest from a $20,000 bank deposit.

With her white superstructure gleaming in the bright morning sunshine, and trailing a thin streamer of gray smoke from her single black stack, the 160-foot *Alice* departed Dawson City June 16, 1897.

Two days later the *Portus B. Weare,* a twin stacker, pulled out. Larger than the *Alice,* 175 feet long with a 38-foot beam, the *Weare* had so much gold stored in her second-deck staterooms that the creaking deck supports had to be shored up to prevent their collapse.

Many of the passengers were shoehorned into double bunks in cubbyhole staterooms measuring only four by six feet. These sternwheelers were built to haul freight to trading posts and mining camps upriver from St. Michael, and passenger comfort was a minor consideration. Some of the miners, distrustful of crew members, spent most of their time playing solitaire in these tiny staterooms while guarding their gold.

An astounding $1,500,000 in Klondike gold left Dawson City on the *Alice* and the *Weare*. The two boats chugged downriver, through the winding loops and curves of the muddy Yukon, crooked as a discarded boot lace.

After stopping briefly at Circle City, an almost deserted mining camp of 300 log cabins, the sternwheelers entered the Yukon Flats, a 200-mile stretch where the river grows shallow. As the wandering currents sloughed away the riverbanks, tall spruce and cottonwood trees toppled into the water, creating hazardous "sweepers" which vessels had to avoid. Ninety miles downstream from Circle City, the riverboats stopped to pick up the mail at Fort Yukon, where the northernmost sweep of the river crosses the Arctic Circle.

On June 23, the *Alice* arrived at St. Michael, a dreary little settlement perched on an island in Norton Sound about 90 miles northeast of the mouth of the Yukon River. Two days later the *Weare* steamed in. The travel-weary miners went ashore in search of fresh fruit and vegetables, but were disappointed because the first ocean steamer of the season had not yet arrived.

They did not have long to wait. After pushing her way through 40 miles of drifting ice floes in the Bering Sea, the steamer *Excelsior,* from San Francisco, anchored off St. Michael on June 30. Four hours later the wooden-hulled *Portland* arrived. While the impatient miners watched from shore, the two vessels discharged their cargo into lighters for the transfer to shore.

Now the miners received their first newspapers since the fall freeze-up. They learned that William McKinley had been inaugurated president, having defeated William Jennings Bryan in the November elections; that Bob Fitzsimmons was the new heavyweight boxing champion of the world, having licked Jim Corbett in a 14-round match at Carson City, Nevada, March 17.

Sixty-eight miners and their gold left St. Michael on the steamer *Portland,* bound for Seattle, 2,700 miles away. A small ship, only 191 feet long and rated at 1,089 gross tons, she had difficulty maintaining a speed of eight knots. Miners unable to obtain accommodations on the *Portland* took the smaller and speedier *Excelsior,* whose destination was San Francisco. Ship's stewards on both vessels received generous tips of gold dust as the men from the Klondike gorged themselves on oranges, apples and raw onions. After an uneventful voyage, the *Excelsior* arrived at San Francisco July 14.

Runners from the leading hotels met the *Excelsior* at the dock. Tom Lippy and three companions commandeered the Palace Hotel carriage and ordered its driver to take them to the United States Mint. When they learned that the mint was closed for a month to take inventory, they directed the driver to transport them and their heavy loads of gold to the Selby Smelting Works. Other miners took over several other hotel carriages and headed for the smelter.

At the Selby Smelting Works, curious onlookers craned their necks and gawked as the miners carried their bags and boxes of gold into the smelter office. After his gold was weighed, each man was handed a receipt. Payment would be made after individual deposits were assayed.

The next day, the San Francisco newspapers carried

widely differing accounts of the men and gold on the *Excelsior*. One newspaper never mentioned the Klondike, stating that the gold came from the Fortymile district. Another newspaper story featured an interview with Mrs. Thomas Lippy and casually mentioned in the concluding paragraph that the *Excelsior* carried nearly half a million dollars in gold.

Under a headline reading "Sacks of Gold from the Clondyke [*sic*]," *The San Francisco Chronicle* ran a front page article two-and-a-half columns long, listing the names of the 15 miners aboard the *Excelsior* and the value of the gold carried by each man.

While news of the astounding amount of Klondike gold aboard the *Excelsior* created considerable excitement in the west, especially among miners and mining promoters, the laconic news dispatches telegraphed to eastern newspapers failed to generate any widespread interest in the Klondike.

One Seattle newspaper handled the arrival of the *Portland* in a more imaginative manner. *The Seattle Post-Intelligencer* chartered the tug *Sea Lion,* ordered staff correspondent Beriah Brown aboard, and sent the tug to intercept the treasure ship as it pulled into Puget Sound.

Boarding the *Portland* on July 17, 1897, at 2 A.M. off Port Angeles, about 60 miles from Seattle, Brown interviewed Captain Sprague and a few of the miners who were up and around. Brown then returned to the *Sea Lion* and wrote his story while the tug sped back to Seattle, arriving at 6 A.M. Story in hand, Brown ran from the pier to the *Post-Intelligencer* office on the northwest corner of Second Avenue and Cherry Street.

At 7:15 A.M., the *Portland* eased up to Schwabacher's Wharf at the foot of Union Street. Only four people were on the wharf when crewmen heaved the lines from the ship to the pier. Three men from the *Post-Intelligencer* helped the night watchman haul in the hawsers: James D. Hoge, one of the owners, and Samuel P. Weston and Arthur W. Whalley of the paper's business office.

At 9 A.M., a special edition of the *Post-Intelligencer* hit the streets. The story of the *Portland* and her gold occupied the entire front page.

ON BOARD STEAMSHIP PORTLAND 3 A.M.
At 3 o'clock this morning the steamship *Portland,* from St. Michael for Seattle, passed up sound with more than a ton of solid gold on board and 68 passengers. In the captain's office are three chests and a large safe filled with precious nuggets. The metal is worth nearly $700,000 and most of it was taken out of the ground in less than three months last winter. In size the nuggets range from the size of a pea to a guinea egg. Of the 68 miners aboard, hardly a man has less than $7,000 and one or two have more than $100,000 in yellow nuggets.[3]

News of the arrival of a ton of gold on the *Portland* rolled through Seattle's downtown business district with the speed and force of a tidal wave. One hour after the *Portland* tied up, hundreds of shouting men jammed Schwabacher's Wharf, shoving one another around as they fought to get a close-up look at the miners and their gold. It became a day of frenzied excitement for most of Seattle's 60,000 citizens. Groups of would-be prospectors huddled together on street corners to exchange information on outfitting for the Yukon.

Intoxicated by the invisible golden halo ringing the *Portland,* workmen quit their jobs and businessmen sold their stores to get started for the Yukon. John McGraw, a former governor of the state of Washington, was one of the 150 passengers on the *Portland* when she left Seattle July 23 to connect at St. Michael with what an advertisement for the North American Transportation and Trading Company described as the "large and elegant *Portus B. Weare.*" Even the mayor of Seattle, William D. Wood, succumbed to the lure of Klondike gold. He resigned his office, purchased a ship and sailed north to go prospecting in the Yukon. Samuel Weston, who had helped to tie up the *Portland* when she docked, also went north. He took with him a dozen carrier pigeons to send dispatches from the Klondike back to his paper.

On the day the *Portland* docked, news correspondents in Seattle telegraphed 20,000 words of copy about the Klondike to eastern and midwestern newspapers. Within a week, news stories on the Klondike and the Yukon were being telegraphed from Seattle at the rate of 50,000 words a day. Newspapers everywhere picked up and echoed the dramatic "ton of gold" phrase originated by reporter Beriah Brown.

A ton of gold! That was the magic phrase, the spark that touched off the stampede to the Klondike. One newsman described the mass madness: "Farmers dropped their plows, bank clerks their ledgers, laborers their picks and shovels, loafers borrowed more money, fathers kissed wife and children goodbye, rich men, poor men and middle men hurried to the railroad station with but one goal in view—the great gold rush was on."[4]

Half a million men started for the Klondike. Only one man in ten had what it took to get there. Four thousand prospectors hacked away at the frozen muck in the ancient creek beds of the Klondike until they found the gold they had come for. Four hundred lucky ones became immensely wealthy. During the next ten years more than $300,000,000 in gold came out of the Klondike.

George Washington Carmack had started it all August 17, 1896, when he picked up a few nuggets of gold and staked his Discovery Claim on Bonanza Creek.

Most newspaper and magazine articles about the Klondike during gold-rush days focused on how to get there and what to bring along. Stories dealing with the discovery made brief mentions of Carmack and his important role, but told nothing of Carmack's younger days. The few journalists who reached Carmack on Bonanza Creek found him a somewhat enigmatic figure with an aversion to interviews. When prodded, he became evasive. There was a youthful indiscretion in his past; he meant to keep it a secret and he did. As a result, the full story of Carmack's family background, his contest with life and the environmental forces that shaped him didn't get into print until half a century after his death, with the publication of this book.

Chapter 2

Young Carmack
Gripped by Gold Fever

George Washington Carmack was born September 24, 1860, in Contra Costa County, California. His parents, Hannah and Perry Carmack, lived on a ranch near Bull Valley, later known as Port Costa. After the birth of her son, Hannah gradually declined in health, and she died when George was three years old. His sister Hannah Rosella—called Rose—was only eight, but she did her best to mother her little brother. She continued to mother him the rest of his life.

When Rose was 14, she married James Watson, who was

Hannah Carmack holding her son George, June 1861 (left) and Perry Carmack, George's father, 1870 (right). (COURTESY ERNEST C. SAFTIG)

38, the same age as her father. Rose had become a tall, thin girl with stringy black hair that reached below her waist. The simple wedding dress she wore, with its complement of billowing petticoats, was the only dowry she brought to her husband.

For several years James Watson had operated a wagon-freighting service between Marysville and the gold mines of the Sierra Nevada. In the fashion of the day, he wore his hair shoulder length. His long, bushy mustache gave him a fiercer look than he deserved.

When Perry Carmack died of apoplexy at the age of 40, his 11-year-old son moved in with sister Rose and her husband. George had just completed the fifth grade at a country school. He liked to read, wrote clearly in a bold hand, made good grades at school and possessed an inquisitive and retentive mind.

Rose wanted her brother to continue his education and study for the Baptist ministry. Her husband would have none of this nonsense; he told George his schooldays were over, and put him to work as a sheepherder, taking care of the Watson flock.

While wagon-freighting to the Sierra Nevada gold diggings, Watson often received gold dust and nuggets in payment. He saved the larger nuggets. On his 12th birthday, George held a dozen nuggets in his hand. The weight of the small chunks of yellow metal astounded the boy. He remained speechless until he handed the nuggets back to Watson.

Rosella (Rose) Carmack, 14, and James Watson, 38, on their wedding day, 1869. (COURTESY ERNEST C. SAFTIG)

"When I grow up, I'm going to be a gold miner," he announced.

"Got the gold bug, eh boy?" replied the man who was the boy's foster father as well as his brother-in-law. "Well, son, you'll do exactly as I tell you until you're 21. After that you can do as you please."

Before long Watson sent the boy out to work at neighboring ranches, where he earned $15 a month as a sheepherder. After eight years of handing his wages over to Watson, George developed an intense dislike of sheepherding and

George Carmack in his Marine Corps uniform, 1881. (COURTESY ERNEST C. SAFTIG)

The U.S.S. Wachusett *at Mare Island, 1881.* (COURTESY NAVAL PHOTOGRAPHIC CENTER, WASHINGTON, D.C.)

ranching. His boyish ambition to become a gold miner remained in his mind, but he realized he lacked the prospecting know-how and grubstake money to start a mining career.

A month after his 21st birthday, no longer subject to James Watson's dictates, George Carmack went to the Mare Island Navy Yard and enlisted in the United States Marine Corps. The medical officer who examined him noted that Carmack was five feet nine inches tall, weighed 160 pounds, had blue eyes, brown hair and a light complexion, and appeared to be in good health. Carmack fit nicely into his Marine Corps uniform; fitting into the rigidly structured routine proved to be irritating, but as time went on he grew more comfortable with military discipline.

In February 1882, Carmack and 23 companions boarded the *U.S.S. Wachusett,* a three-masted sailing vessel equipped with an auxiliary steam engine. Bound for Sitka to maintain peace and order in Southeastern Alaska, the *Wachusett* sailed through the Golden Gate and into the

Parade ground at Sitka, 1880s. The Marine Corps barracks at right,
U.S. Customs House at lower left, and "Baranov's Castle" at upper
left. (COURTESY ALASKA HISTORICAL LIBRARY, JUNEAU)

open sea.

After a rough 15-day voyage, the *Wachusett* arrived at
Sitka and anchored in the island-studded harbor. Carmack
leaned against the main deck rail for his first glimpse of the
little settlement sprawled along the curving beach. On one
side of the wharf, perched atop a rocky promontory rising a
hundred feet above the water, stood "Baranov's Castle," a
massive, moss-covered structure built of squared cedar
logs. On the other side of the wharf stretched a large parade
ground, bordered by the beach and the three-story Marine
barracks. Snow-covered peaks towered behind the town
like painted scenery in a theater backdrop.

Every morning the Marines turned out for inspection.
Weekly marching drills were held on the parade ground.
Marine discipline relaxed during off-duty hours, and
Carmack used his leisure time to explore the town, only a
few steps away from the barracks.

The Tlingit Indians lived in an area known as the
"rancherie," separated from the town by a tall cedar fence.
At night, a gate was locked to keep the Tlingits away from

the townpeople. Carmack enjoyed talking with the Tlingits and soon picked up the Chinook jargon the Indians used to communicate with white men. Carmack then turned his attention to the Tlingit dialect, learning enough of that guttural language to carry on an ordinary conversation. He seemed to have a natural flair for new languages.

During the spring of 1882, dozens of idle prospectors and gold miners tramped the muddy streets of Sitka, some coming from the Cassiar gold fields of British Columbia, drawn to Sitka by news of the recent gold discoveries in Juneau and elsewhere in Alaska. A year earlier, some of them had crossed over the Chilkoot Pass into the upper Yukon valley where they found a smattering of fine gold along some of the Yukon tributaries. Now they were wintering in Sitka, awaiting the spring breakup of ice on the lakes and rivers of the interior before venturing into the Yukon again.

Chatting with miners he met in the bars of Sitka, Carmack's gold fever broke out anew. Only his Marine Corps obligation prevented him from grabbing pick and pan and heading for the hills to search for gold.

In the fall of 1882, the *U.S.S. Adams* and a new contingent of Marines relieved the *Wachusett*. Carmack and the other Marines boarded the *Wachusett* to return home. After a voyage pounded by autumn gales, the ship reached San Francisco Bay in mid-October and anchored off Mare Island.

A few days after the *Wachusett* arrived, Carmack received a letter from James Watson and learned that Rose had pneumonia. The ship's captain, Commander Frederick Pearson, U.S.N., denied Carmack's request for shore leave and ordered the entire ship's complement to remain aboard, causing considerable resentment. By early November more than one-third of the ship's Marines had been logged for being absent without leave. Carmack was one of 15 men who left the ship and never returned.

Pleased to be back home with Rose and James Watson at their ranch near Cambria, California, and delighted to learn of his sister's steady improvement, Carmack explained why he had left his ship. Rose begged him to return. George refused. He wanted to go north again to prospect for gold in Alaska or the Yukon. But first, he must save up more money.

Carmack hired out as a sheepherder for a rancher in the Modesto area. His wages of $25 a month were a bit higher than the $17.50 he had earned as a Marine. He wrote regularly to Rose, who always replied promptly. In one letter she gently admonished him.

> You must think twice before you jump again, dear brother, and not be so rash the next time. I wish you would hurry and sow your wild oats and settle down with me, for I am proud of my big brother when he is good. You don't know how earnestly I pray that you will not walk in forbidden paths.[1]

In December 1883, while sheepherding near Tulare, a lonely Carmack pulled out his pocket diary and wrote a little verse.

My Thoughts

On Tulare plains amongst alkaline weeds,
Or rich wet grass where the wild goose feeds,
My mind far o'er the hills does roam,
Back to the joys and comforts of home.
To the fern-clad hills and the grand old pine,
And the dogwood blossoms and the rose-bush vine.
The songs of the birds and the hum of the bee,
And the old log house in fancy I see.[2]

By the spring of 1885, Carmack had saved almost $500, enough to get started north. He made plans to leave for Juneau, where he would outfit for a summer of prospecting in Alaska or the Yukon. On March 29, he said goodbye to Rose and James, and to his girlfriend, Becky, and left for San Francisco. With his steamship ticket in his shirt pocket, a roll of bills in his pants pocket and gold fever in his blood, he felt confident of his future.

The *Queen of the Pacific,* with Captain E. Alexander on the bridge, pulled away from the Broadway Wharf

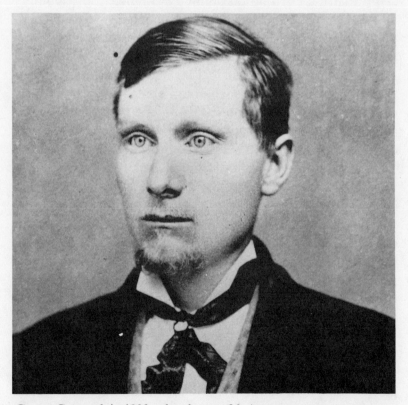

George Carmack in 1883, when he was 23. (COURTESY ERNEST C. SAFTIG)

promptly at 10 A.M. March 31. She was a new ship, only three years old. Carmack had purchased steerage quarters in the bow and saw little of her luxurious appointments. He stayed on deck while the vessel passed through the Golden Gate and into the North Pacific Ocean. As the ship corkscrewed into the big swells, Carmack listened to the slapping waves and sniffed the salty air. He was glad to be at sea again.

After a brief stop at Astoria, Oregon, the *Queen of the Pacific* docked at Victoria, British Columbia, to discharge a cargo that included 3,000 pounds of opium, 3,015 pounds of tobacco, 12,500 pounds of black powder and 54,357 pounds of sugar. When the *Queen* arrived at her final destination, Port Townsend in Washington Territory, George Carmack and other passengers for Alaska were transferred to the steamer *Idaho,* a smaller and older vessel. Under the command of Captain James Carroll, the *Idaho* made a fast and uneventful voyage up the Inland Passage to the Southeastern Alaska towns of Wrangell, Sitka and Juneau City.

The *Idaho* slowed as she approached Juneau City on a rainy April day. Three long blasts of the ship's whistle echoed from the dark, forested mountainsides and reverberated down fjord-like Gastineau Channel. Carmack came out on deck for his first glimpse of the little gold-mining camp. He saw a scraggly collection of log cabins and unpainted frame buildings plastered against a steep mountain slope. Flocks of gray and white herring gulls screeched as they circled the ship, while dozens of sea birds paddled briskly in the water, escorting the *Idaho* to the wharf.

As the *Idaho* tied up, rubber-booted white men on the small wharf good-naturedly jostled one another. Wearing garish combinations of white man's clothing, a few Auke Indian men stood barefoot in the rain, and blanket-wrapped Auke women, some with blackened faces, huddled

Juneau in 1886. The vessel just off the wharf is the S.S. Idaho; *smoke across the channel comes from the Treadwell Mine.* (COURTESY ALASKA HISTORICAL LIBRARY, JUNEAU)

together, chatting in low, guttural phrases.

With his pack on his back, Carmack walked down the gangplank and stepped cautiously along the slippery, wet planks of the wharf until he reached Front Street, a muddy, two-rut road that followed the curve of the beach. The incessant Juneau rain dripped from his wide-brimmed hat like a miniature waterfall. He followed the other passengers along a wooden sidewalk barely wide enough to accommodate two people walking side by side.

As the gusty wind swept down from the wooded slopes of the mountain, it carried the heavy, moist tang of spruce trees, an odor more agreeable than the fishy stink of the beach at low tide. Ravens croaked dismally as if protesting the raucous screaming of the gulls.

Carmack kept going until he reached a hotel, where he rented a room. After dinner he wandered in and out of several saloons that served as social clubs for the 600 residents of the camp. In two hours, he met no one he had known at Sitka, and returned to his hotel.

Next morning, Carmack walked up the Gold Creek trail to look at the placer diggings. The creek was at flood stage, swollen by heavy rains and melting snow from the mountain basins above. He talked with a miner shoveling gravel into a sluice box. No, he wasn't doing very well. Yes, the paydirt had petered out. During the past four years the Gold Creek placers had produced more than half a million dollars in gold. Now they were barren and empty.

When he returned to his hotel, Carmack nodded a greeting to the friendly hotel manager who was engaged in a lively conversation with two middle-aged men.

"Mr. Carmack, shake hands with Hugh Day and Albert Day. These two brothers prospected in the Yukon last summer. They must have found something, 'cause they're going back."

Carmack was thrilled by the fascinating story told by the talkative Day brothers. The two French-Canadians had staked a rich placer claim in the Cassiar district of British Columbia, made a sizable chunk of money and then sold out. In the summer of 1884 the brothers had prospected on several tributaries of the upper Yukon, finding flour gold on many river bars but no nuggets or coarse gold. With a third partner, Isaac Powers, they were now outfitting in Juneau for another prospecting venture into the Yukon. An inquisitive Carmack asked many questions.

"How long you fellows plan to stay in the Yukon?"

Al Day replied while his brother lit his pipe.

"One year. We'll winter on the Stewart River. There's coarse gold there. We didn't find any, but some other fellows did."

"How will you get there?"

"We'll get somebody with a boat to take us to the mouth of the Taiya River, about 120 miles north of here. Then we'll hire Indian packers to carry our outfit over the

Chilkoot Pass trail to Lake Lindemann, about 25 miles. At the lake we'll build a boat big enough to carry the three of us and supplies for a year. When the ice goes out, we'll paddle or sail down the chain of lakes until we reach the Yukon. Then we'll drift down to the mouth of the Stewart."

"Why the Indian packers?" Carmack asked.

Al Day smiled at the eagerness of the cheechako seated beside him. "That climb over the Chilkoot Pass is terrible. It's a real man-killer. Besides, it would take the three of us more than a month to move our 2,000-pound outfit over the pass. We can hire 30 or 40 packers and get the whole she-bang moved over to Lake Lindemann in two or three days. Then we'll have plenty of time to build our boat before the ice goes out 'bout the end of May."

"Got room for one more man?" asked Carmack, his blue eyes shining with excitement.

"No. Tell you what, though. You line up a couple of other fellows to go with you. Hugh and I'll help you get an outfit together. You can travel with us going over the Chilkoot Pass trail."

"That's good enough for me," said Carmack as he shook hands with his new trail partners.

Within a week, Carmack had persuaded three other adventurers to join him for a summer of prospecting in the Yukon. They were Hugh Donahue, J.V. Dawson and D. Foley, none of whom had ever been in the Yukon. While the Day party had no money problems, the Carmack group was not so fortunate. Each of the four partners put up $200, which was thrown into a common pot to buy supplies and equipment. They agreed that Carmack, the most talkative and enthusiastic member, would be the leader of the expedition. Any gold found during the summer would be divided equally among the four partners. It was a bold venture for a group with so little prospecting knowledge or experience, but frontier prospectors are inherently optimistic, and every man in Carmack's party firmly believed he would find a fortune in gold in the Yukon.

To reduce expenses, Carmack moved out of the hotel and set up housekeeping in a tent. The next day his partners moved in with him. They dug clams on the beach and bought salmon or halibut from the Indians at ten cents a fish. When the fish diet became monotonous, Carmack, the only man with a rifle, went hunting and brought back a deer.

According to the Day brothers, there were no trading posts along the upper Yukon, so everything necessary for the success of the venture had to be purchased in Juneau. Carmack and his partners bought enough flour, bacon, beans, baking powder, tea and other food staples to last them three months. They bought saws, axes, nails, pitch and oakum to be used in the construction of their boat. By the time they were ready to go, their outfit weighed more than 800 pounds. At Hugh Day's suggestion, they laid in a supply of gold and silver coins to pay the Indian packers, who would not accept paper money.

Since there was no scheduled freight or passenger service to the Taiya River, obtaining boat transportation to that isolated spot turned out to be a problem. A pair of Auke Indians offered to move the prospectors and their outfits wherever they wanted to go, but their slim dugout canoes seemed much too fragile for the long trip up Lynn Canal. The solution came from an unexpected source.

Early on the morning of May 14, the *U.S.S. Pinta,* a gunboat usually stationed at Sitka, arrived at Juneau. Some natives from the Indian village near Chilkoot (now Haines), had gone on a drunken shooting spree, and fired on white men living in the area. The *Pinta* had been ordered to investigate, and apprehend the guilty ones if they could be found. When Al Day learned that only a dozen miles or so separated Chilkoot from the Taiya River, he boarded the *Pinta* and persuaded her captain, Lieutenant Commander Henry E. Nichols, U.S.N., to transport the seven men and their outfits to Chilkoot. Before it could leave, however, the *Pinta* was obliged to await the arrival of the *Idaho,* which carried a cargo of coal. After the coal was loaded aboard the *Pinta,* the Day and Carmack parties and their supplies were taken aboard.

The *Pinta* left Juneau at 6 A.M. Saturday, May 16, 1885. Her fore and aft sails were raised to take advantage of a favorable wind, but soon had to be hauled down to keep them from being burned by hot gases from the galley's stove pipe.

Aboard the *Pinta* were two sailors who had served on the *Wachusett* with Carmack in 1882. Despite the bushy mustache and beard Carmack had grown, his widely spaced

The U.S.S. Pinta *in Juneau harbor, 1889.* (COURTESY NAVAL PHOTOGRAPHIC CENTER, WASHINGTON, D.C.)

eyes and prominent nose were unmistakable. His former shipmates recognized him immediately, but did not reveal his identity. The three enjoyed a brief reunion, reminiscing about their experiences together on the *Wachusett*.

Late in the afternoon, the *Pinta* dropped anchor off the village of Chilkoot. When the captain learned that neither Dawson nor Donahue owned a rifle, he directed that each man be issued a Springfield rifle and 250 rounds of ball cartridge. The men signed receipts and promised to return the rifles when they came back to Juneau in the fall.

Early Tuesday morning, May 19, the *Pinta*'s two steam launches departed, ferrying the men and their supplies to the Taiya River. They were greeted at the mouth of the river that afternoon by myriad tiny mosquitoes with ravenous appetites.

"Only 25 miles to Lake Lindemann," shouted Carmack as he rubbed his swollen nose and swatted the bugs. "Let's get going!"

Chapter 3

Into the Yukon

As the launches from the *Pinta* faded from sight in the slanting rain of a passing squall, the prospectors made camp for the night. Carmack and his partners were putting up their tent when a big Indian canoe with upturned prow came gliding up to the shore. Three Indians climbed over the ornate bow decorated with carved totemic figures and walked slowly up the sloping beach.

"Must be the Chilkoot packers," said Al Day. "Anybody here savvy Chinook?"

"Nika kumtux Chinook," replied Carmack. "I understand Chinook. Learned the lingo at Sitka."

"George, you dicker for our party. All I know about Chinook is that 'klahowya' means 'how are you'."

"Leave it to me."

"Don't take their first offer. Last year we paid $15 a hundred; that's too much."

"I've haggled with Indians before," Carmack responded testily.

"Klahowya," said the tall Indian with the stringy mustache.

"Klahowya," replied Carmack.

"Mika kumtux Chinook?"

"Nika kumtux Chinook."

Al Day was right: These men were Indian packers from a nearby village. Long before the first white men went over the pass and disappeared into the Yukon country, the Chilkoots were using the Chilkoot Pass trail. Every summer they crossed the pass to trade with the Indians of the interior, swapping their seal and fish oil for the furs of the Tagish and other tribes along the Yukon. The Chilkoots knew exactly where the icy-cold Taiya River could be safely forded and where the best overnight shelter could be found.

The spokesman for the Indians offered to pack the Day and Carmack outfits over the pass to Lake Lindemann for $15 a hundred pounds. Carmack countered with an opening offer of five dollars. After an hour of friendly dickering, Carmack and the Indian leader agreed the packers would receive eight dollars per hundred. In addition, each packer would be given one cup of flour daily to supplement the dried salmon he took along for food. Carmack agreed to have all the supplies and equipment put up in bundles or boxes weighing less than 100 pounds each. The Chilkoots would supply 40 packers for the Day group and eight packers for the Carmack party.

Carmack was up early the following morning, eager to get under way. When the Chilkoot packers arrived, they laughed and shouted jovially as they poked at the bundles with their fingers or prodded them with walking sticks. They were searching for soft, pliant loads such as bacon or flour, which could be carried more comfortably than cans or boxes with sharp corners.

The Chilkoots were one of the fiercest and most aggressive branches of the Tlingit Indians. Short and stocky with thick chests, massive heads and pale brown faces, the packers swarmed around their leader, the tallest of the lot, who assigned the loads. Four boys, ten or 12 years old, were each given packs of 50 pounds. Eight women, some wearing half a dozen silver bracelets on their arms, carried 75-pound sacks. The men each received packs weighing from 75 to 120 pounds.

Carmack noticed that the heaviest load was given to a one-eyed young Chilkoot wearing a patched woolen shirt, a small black cap, a headband strap and ragged denim trousers held up with a sinew cord. On his back, cushioned by a blanket, he carried two 50-pound sacks of flour topped with a 20-pound slab of bacon. As did most of his companions, he carried a stout walking stick.

Each Chilkoot woman wore a long full skirt, a cape-like blanket draped over her shoulders and a kerchief covering her head. Both men and women favored native moccasins reaching well above the ankle. Only the white men wore rain clothing.

By nine o'clock the Chilkoots had started up the trail. The long column had traveled less than a mile when it moved past the one-building settlement of Dyea. Founder John J. Healy stood in the doorway of the Healy & Wilson Trading Post and greeted the white men as they passed.

Carmack found it difficult to keep up with the Indians

with an 80-pound load on his back. After traveling six miles over a rocky and hilly trail, his pack straps were digging into his shoulders and his feet hurt. He welcomed the stop for lunch. The white men refreshed themselves with tea and warmed-up bacon cooked the night before; the Chilkoots chewed dried salmon and drank water from a creek. Clouds of mosquitoes lunched on both groups.

Up to this point, the trail had stuck close to the winding Taiya River, now a noisy, white-water torrent. Early in the afternoon, the expedition reached a fork in the stream, where the Nourse River empties into the Taiya. The packers followed the smaller Taiya, heading northeasterly toward Chilkoot Pass. Once again, the procession forded the glacier-fed river and detoured around a mile-long canyon with steep, rocky sides. Before stopping for the night, the hardy Chilkoots pushed on for another four miles. The party had passed the halfway point but the steepest and most difficult climb was still ahead.

They camped in a wide valley where the spruce forest came down to the edge of the river. Pitchy dead spruce boughs were plentiful, and soon the campfires sent forth a tear-producing smoke that kept both men and mosquitoes at a distance. Carmack and his white companions put up tents; the Chilkoots slept under the trees. Since many of the Chilkoots were insatiable gamblers, they soon had a game going, playing with bone markers and keeping score with willow sticks.

After supper Carmack took off his leather boots, wrung out his socks and hung them to dry. Stretching out by the fire, he lit his pipe and watched a lone eagle circling overhead. Then, weary, he crawled into his tent and went to sleep.

The sturdy Chilkoots, gamblers and all, arose early. Their shouting awakened Carmack. Stiff and aching all over, he emerged slowly from his tent. Frost covered the ground. Huge gray clouds concealed the mountain peaks on both sides of the valley but not the fresh snow on the slopes below.

The party got off to an early start. The Indians wanted to get over the snow-covered approach to the summit before the midday sun turned the crusted snow into slippery slush. A two-mile climb along a trail that zigzagged across several outcroppings of bedrock brought them to an area where boulders big as cabins had tumbled into the stream. Now well above timberline, they slogged along in the crunchy snow, then rested briefly at the base of the cliff-like slope just below a notch in the mountains.

With zealous heart but aching feet, Carmack slipped back into his shoulder straps and adjusted his pack before beginning the final ascent to the crest of the Chilkoot Pass. Between him and the summit loomed a massive, snow-covered rock slide, sloping upward at a 40° angle for a quarter of a mile. Clinging to the corner of a projecting boulder, he pulled himself up as his feet groped for a foothold. His fingers were soon numbed by the cold, and occasionally his leg muscles cramped as he crawled up the creviced surface of the rocky mass. Climbing on all fours, lifting himself by sheer willpower when muscle-power faltered, Carmack struggled toward the top. He marveled at the agility and endurance of the Chilkoots crossing the wind-whipped slope. It took him almost an hour to reach the rim of the summit, but as he lay panting and sweating in the snow, a feeling of triumph and achievement surged through him.

Since wood for a fire was not available on the treeless crest, Indians and white men alike ate a cold meal as they rested.

"We still in Alaska?" Carmack asked.

"Nope. We're in Canada," Al Day replied. "The

Chilkoot Pass is right on the boundary. Watch this." He picked up a snowball and threw it down the steep slope they had just climbed. "When that snowball melts, the water will go down the Taiya and reach salt water right where we started from, only 15 miles from here."

He scooped up another snowball, which he threw in the opposite direction. "When that one melts, the water will flow down through a chain of lakes until it gets to the Yukon River. Then it will have to go a couple of thousand miles before it gets to the Bering Sea."

After sloshing down through a steep bank of soft snow, digging their heels in to keep from sliding, the packers reached Crater Lake, which was still frozen. Here, the terrain flattened out to a gentler slope, making traveling easier. They pushed on until nine that night, when they reached the shore of Lake Lindemann. Setting down their loads, the packers demanded their pay. Right after supper, Carmack and his exhausted companions went to sleep; the hardy Chilkoots resumed their stick gambling games.

In the morning, the Indians departed for Dyea while the Day and Carmack parties began searching for timber suitable for boat building. Unlike the tall, thick trees of the coastal regions, the stunted spruce nearby were short and thin.

The ice on Lake Lindemann measured more than a foot thick. Hugh Day estimated it would be another ten days or so before the ice would break up and start moving northward.

Meanwhile, the Day brothers introduced Carmack and his partners to another backbreaking experience: whipsawing logs into lumber. They began by erecting an elevated platform of logs. Ten feet square, it was supported by vertical posts at each corner. A log incline was built on one side of the platform. The logs to be sawn were first stripped of their bark, then pushed up the incline to the platform. One man on the platform and his partner on the ground below worked the saw up and down as they cut one-inch boards.

The work was hard and tiring. Tempers flared often, especially when the man on the ground received a shower of sawdust down his neck. Carmack found it difficult to keep the saw straight, resulting in boards of uneven thickness.

The Carmack party planned a boat 20 feet long by five feet wide; the Day brothers' would be larger. Each would have a flat bottom, square stern and flared sides. There was no time to dry the lumber, so as fast as the boards were cut, the edges were planed smooth and the boards were nailed into position. Carmack pounded oakum into the seams and sealed them with heated pitch.

On May 30, the prospectors cheered as they watched the huge blocks of ice break up and drift through patches of open water toward the lake's outlet. The next day, the two groups launched their boats, prepared to go their separate ways.

The Day brothers wanted to reach the mouth of the Stewart River, almost 500 miles distant, as soon as possible.

Carmack and his three partners spent a week along the creeks that emptied into Lake Bennett, a 30-mile-long lake just a few miles from Lake Lindemann. Only an occasional glint of gold appeared when they panned the stream gravels on the east side, but near the northern end of the lake, at a point where three small creeks converged, they found the first showing of fine gold dust.

After drifting through the narrow channel connecting the northern end of Lake Bennett with Nares Lake, the men paddled north into Lake Tagish. Once again, they found nothing more encouraging than an occasional showing of color.

On the Fourth of July, the prospectors were camped on

the eastern shore of Lake Marsh, another lake in the chain. While his partners prospected, Carmack went in search of fresh meat, bagging two rabbits.

Later, the expedition ascended the McClintock River for a few miles (Carmack called it Crooked River on the crude map he drew). The sands of the river's larger gravel bars yielded fairly good showings of flour gold.

After a week of constant prospecting, the four men had collected several ounces of fine gold dust but no coarse gold or nuggets. Although they found flour gold on almost every gravel bar they panned, they had not found enough in one spot to warrant staking a claim.

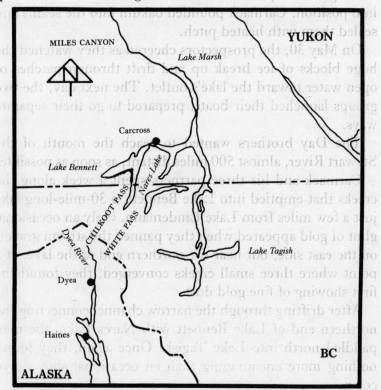

Southern lakes region of the Yukon.

Carmack found the life of the prospector as alluring and satisfying as he had dreamed it would be. He enjoyed the isolation of the Yukon wilderness, and the hope of striking a bonanza on the next gravel bar never left him. His failure to find substantial quantities of gold in any of the dozens of river bars he panned did not lessen his satisfaction or weaken his determination to keep trying.

As their boat drifted down the Lewes River, (now also called the Yukon) the outlet of Lake Marsh, Carmack and his partners washed out endless pans of gravel from the bars of the smaller tributaries. They found colors almost everywhere, some flour gold, but nothing larger than a few flecks the size of a pinhead. The only game of any size that Carmack sighted were a few mountain goats, all of them on inaccessible mountain slopes. By the time the men reached Miles Canyon—near the site of Whitehorse today—dwindling food supplies made them realize it was time to turn back.

The return trip was slow as the men paddled, poled and towed their boat upstream. At the southern end of Lake Bennett, they cached the boat and continued on foot. Traveling light, they made good time on the Chilkoot Trail. By the first week of August they were back in Juneau.

After a bath and a shave at the hotel, Carmack hurried to the post office. His girl Becky had sent him a brief note; the newsy letters from Rose were much longer. Carmack waited two weeks before writing back to his sister.

He described his 150-mile journey into the Yukon and said his share of the gold amounted to only 2 ounces. He reported to Rose on his health and expressed his confidence in the Yukon.

> I have been well so far, all but a couple of boils, one on
> my toe and one by the side of a corn. The boil and the

Map drawn by George Carmack in a letter to Rose, showing camping places during his 1885 prospecting trip. (PHOTOGRAPH BY M.C. JUNG)

corn had a terrible fight to see which would get the toe, but I think the boil is licked. There is a big gold field in the Yukon, and I want my share of it and am going to have it if the Lord wills it.[1]

Carmack knew he'd have to work to get his share.

> Some men have come up here expecting to find gold laying around on the beach and some of them has got fooled pretty hard. But I have done better than I expected the first year. One young man drowned himself and another shot himself because someone did not fill his pockets with nuggets the day they landed, so you see that gives the country a bad name.[2]

On the back of the last sheet of his letter, Carmack drew a rough map indicating the places where his party had camped and the spots where they had found traces of gold.

Chapter 4

Carmack Meets a Tagish Girl

Work was scarce in Juneau during the autumn of 1885, and Carmack was unable to find a steady job. He applied at the Treadwell Mine on nearby Douglas Island, only to be turned away, as were dozens of other men who stood in line with him.

Carmack was not idle; he shot deer on the mountain meadows above Juneau, packed them into town and sold them for four dollars each. By October, though, heavy snow had driven the deer away.

With no money coming in, Carmack moved out of the

hotel, which had cost him five dollars a week, and set up a tent on the outskirts of town. He shot ducks and geese on the tidal flats. When spawning salmon disappeared from the streams, he fished for bottomfish and dug clams on the beach. A steady diet of fish and clams grew monotonous, and his tent proved cold and damp.

Gabbing with other idle prospectors during the long winter evenings, Carmack learned that during the past summer, some miners had made as much as $100 a day sluicing gold from the gravel bars of the Stewart, where his friends the Day brothers were wintering. Rumor had it that more than $100,000 in gold had been mined on the Stewart during the summer of 1885. Perhaps he had not gone downriver far enough, Carmack thought; next time would be different. He tightened his resolve to get enough money for a grubstake and another season of prospecting.

On occasional days of despair, Carmack was lonely for home and family and thought of returning to California. He told Rose of his feelings in a November letter.

> I have not been doing much as I can get nothing to do. If I can find enough clams to keep me through the winter I will be solid. Some of the men came back from the Yukon reporting good diggings there. But I don't think I will go in there again. If I can get good wages here in Juneau I will stay until I can make a grubstake for Becky and me."[1]

On the back of this letter, Carmack wrote a message in Chinook jargon, accompanied by a translation in English.

Chinook	English
Nika sick tumtum nika	I am lonesome for I
tika nanitch mika	want to see you.

41

Spose nika iskum	If I make
chickamin nika coolie	some money I will go
nika illahee nanitch	home to see
mika. Spose mika tika	you. I you want
cultus coolie klosh	to go on a pleasure trip
mika chako kopa	you come to
Juneau nanitch nika	Juneau to see me.

The next steamer from Seattle brought Carmack letters from his sister but none from his girl. After two months without a letter from her, Carmack wrote to Rose asking what happened to Becky. Rose replied that Becky was going steady with someone else. Carmack crumpled the letter and threw it on the fire.

"I'm not going to stew about Becky any more," he said aloud. "I'm going back to the Yukon and strike it rich. Then when I get back to California, loaded down with nuggets, she'll be sorry."

By the time pink blossoms again covered the salmonberry bushes, Carmack's impatience to start for the Yukon had increased. Juneau was swarming with prospectors like himself who were stranded on Poverty Rock. Unable to wangle a grubstake on credit, and with only $75 in his pocket, Carmack decided to go up to Dyea, and try to join some prospecting outfit as a guide. If all else failed, he would go to work as a packer.

It cost him ten dollars to get himself and his few belongings transported to Dyea by Indian canoe. He pitched his tent near the Healy & Wilson Trading Post, a large, two-story, hewn-log building, still the only structure at Dyea. Carmack found life here more agreeable than at Juneau. Fish were plentiful, and deer appeared on the beaches almost every morning. Occasionally, he bought tea or tobacco at the trading post, but he had no other cash outlays.

John Healy, a crusty old Irishman with a white mustache and goatee, seemed glad to have another white man to chat with. The Chilkoot Indians, several hundred of whom lived in villages near Dyea, resented the trader's presence in their territory. Healy had nothing but contempt for the Chilkoots, calling them liars, cheats and thieves. He refused to sell them molasses or lemon extract, knowing that they would drink the extract and use the molasses to make a crude alcoholic drink known as "hoochinoo". The other supplies he would sell to anyone. He would accept payment in cash, in gold dust and in furs, but not in the future. Most of his fur trade came from the Tagish Indians of the upper Yukon, who crossed the Chilkoot Pass to deal with him.

One rainy May afternoon, while Carmack chatted with Healy, waiting for Yukon-bound prospectors to show up, two young Indian men entered the store, each carrying a bundle of furs.

"Klahowya, Jim, klahowya, Charley," Healy said.

The Indians acknowledged the greeting with similar expressions and then dumped their furs on the counter.

"George, I want you to meet a couple of honest Indians," Healy said. "This big fellow here is Skookum Jim. He's a Tagish Indian from the interior. He's the best damn packer there is. He can lug a 150-pound load over the pass. That's why they call him Skookum Jim."

Carmack shook hands with the stocky Indian, whose frowning expression never changed.

"This little fellow is Tagish Charley. He's a nephew of Jim's. I got two other Charleys trading with me so I call this one Tagish Charley. The Chilkoots don't like him. They call him Cultus Charley, a no-good Charley, but he's a good packer and tough as a spruce knot."

Carmack watched Healy sort the mass of marten, fox, muskrat and beaver pelts into separate piles. The trader ran his hand expertly over each fur, appraising it. Then the bargaining began, conducted entirely in Chinook. Carmack had no difficulty following it. When the bargaining ended, Skookum Jim received $125 and Tagish Charley agreed to $100. The two Indians told Healy they were looking for work as packers. He suggested they set up camp near Carmack in back of the trading post. The two Tagish men felt that here they were not likely to be harassed by the Chilkoots, who had dominated and terrorized their tribe for many years. Carmack helped them build a crude lean-to of spruce boughs to keep out the summer rain. Having them as neighbors gave Carmack an opportunity to practise his Chinook.

One week later the three men broke camp to start out on the first packing job of the year. This season the packers demanded and got ten dollars for each hundred pounds carried over the trail to Lake Lindemann. Carmack, the only white man packing with the Indians, soon learned that a hundred-pound pack was too much for him. Skookum Jim offered to relieve him of a 20-pound bag of rice; Carmack accepted gladly.

As they struggled up the steep, rocky slope just below the summit of the Chilkoot Pass, Skookum Jim and Tagish Charley stayed close to Carmack, giving him a helping hand now and then. Heavy rain fell during the final ascent, making the snow-covered boulders slippery. It was the most exhausting physical labor Carmack had ever faced, but when he reached the summit, he felt once again a sense of exultation.

The following evening the three men reached Lake Lindemann; two days later they were back at Dyea.

During the summer of 1886, more than 200 prospectors passed through Dyea on their way to the Yukon. Carmack and his two Tagish friends had all the packing jobs they could handle. By August the season had ended. Prospectors from the Yukon began straggling back over the pass to Dyea.

When Skookum Jim and Tagish Charley prepared to return to their village at the foot of Lake Tagish, they urged Carmack to spend the winter with them. Carmack had visited the area on his 1885 prospecting trip; he accepted their invitation. They purchased winter supplies of tea, tobacco and ammunition, said goodbye to Healy, and started over the pass.

Once again at the summit, they put down their packs and rested. It was one of those rare days when the sun shone from a cloudless sky. On all sides, jagged mountain peaks of the coastal range stood out in bold relief. Carmack pointed to the lakes visible in the distance. He was not the only one impressed with the magnificent view. Skookum Jim swung his arm in a wide arc and then spoke, using a combination of Chinook and English.

"Dis Inchen illahee. Hiyu skookum illahee. Hiyu clean, all same sky."

"Yes, Jim, it's Indian country. It's a good land. Plenty clean, like the sky," agreed Carmack.[2]

When the warm winds of summer brush across the jagged backbone of the continental divide at the Chilkoot Pass, countless rivulets of melted snow race down the northern sides of the mountain slopes, gathering together at Crater Lake. Through a hundred-mile chain of lakes, the chilly waters of Crater Lake drift slowly northward as they begin their 2,200-mile journey down the Yukon valley to the Bering Sea. The streams linking the lakes together grow in size and swiftness as the milky waters pass through Long Lake, Deep Lake and Lake Lindemann before reaching Lake Bennett.

At the northern end of Lake Bennett, a short, shallow

stream of swift water 200 yards wide empties into Nares Lake. Every year, hundreds of caribou cross this neck-like channel, going north in June, returning again in September. The migratory movements of the caribou provided good hunting for the band of Indians who lived at the Tagish village, only 15 miles from the caribou crossing. It was here at the Tagish village that Skookum Jim and Tagish Charley were born and grew up.

After the steep descent to Crater Lake, the going became easier as the trail followed a series of rocky ridges, with swampy ground in the hollows. Now Carmack no longer lagged behind his companions. When the trio reached Lake Bennett, they uncovered and launched the boat the two Tagish men had cached in the brush.

The Tagish village was about 50 miles to the north, on the left bank of the river-like channel that connects Lake Tagish with Lake Marsh. On the wide terrace before him, Carmack saw two community houses, built of rough planks, and a dozen smaller log cabins. The Tagish were a small band of Indians, only about 20 families, numbering no more than 70 or 80 in all. A semi-nomadic people, they wandered up and down the Yukon valley as far as Fort Selkirk every summer, returning to their lake site in the fall.

Because only a few Tagish understood Chinook, Carmack had difficulty communicating until he picked up a smattering of their language; it had much in common with the Tlingit language used by the coastal Indians. The Tagish could not pronounce the letter "r"—it is not used in Tagish or Chinook jargon—so when Skookum Jim said "George," it sounded more like "Judge," and the word "river" came out "wiva." In the village, Jim was known by his Tagish name, Kahse.

Carmack joined the Tagish men on their fall hunting trips, where his expert marksmanship quickly earned respect. Whenever a moose or caribou was killed, the carcass went to the village, not to the hunter making the lucky shot. Each family received a chunk of meat, and everyone joined in feasting. The women dried and smoked the surplus meat for use during the winter.

Carmack accompanied Jim and Charley to the men-only tribal dances, where participants wore painted wooden masks and caribou skin robes, elaborately decorated with bear, wolf and raven figures.

After the lakes and rivers froze, the Indians discarded the rag-tag clothing of the white man in favor of the warmer native garments. Carmack followed suit. He had long ago given up his leather boots for knee-high caribou-skin moccasins. Now he put on tight-fitting trousers of caribou skin, worn fur-side in, and a knee-length parka, also of caribou skin. His cap and mittens were made of rabbit skin.

Carmack lived with Jim and his family in one of the big community houses where Jim's aging mother was matriarch. The other occupants of Jim's compartment were his two younger sisters, whose Indian names Carmack could not master. The older sister, tall and slender, he called Jennie. The younger one, whose Tagish name sounded something like Jeef-lot, he called Kate. She was then about 20, with large, doe-like eyes and long hair black as a raven's wing, and Carmack considered that she was the prettiest girl in the village. He wondered why Kate had no husband and concluded that the high-spirited girl felt none of the Tagish men were good enough for her.

Kate did most of the cooking for the family. Carmack grew fond of one Tagish delicacy, smoked caribou tongue, but not until he learned to spit out all the caribou hairs.

Usually Kate went about her household duties cheerfully, but at times the hot-tempered girl indulged in childish tantrums, screaming and railing at anyone who came near.

There was no privacy in Jim's crowded compartment. A bucket in one corner served as a toilet, and everyone slept on the floor. Sometimes Kate smiled at Carmack as she crawled into her bearskin sleeping robe, not far from his own. As he watched her, night after night, Carmack made many a futile wish.

Kate's oldest sister, who lived in the other big community house, had ten children: one girl and the rest boys. Tagish Charley, the oldest boy, looked after his younger brothers, including Kulsin, only six or seven.

Carmack adapted easily to the Tagish way of life. He fished, hunted and trapped, all Indian style. Jim showed him how to make snowshoes, using spruce branches for frames and cutting webbing from caribou hide. With Jim's help, Carmack learned how to set traps for fox, wolf, lynx and other fur-bearing animals. After the spring thaw they caught dozens of muskrats and a few beaver.

With the approach of summer, Carmack realized that he had seen the Yukon country in all its seasons. Following the rhythms of nature, the Tagish hunted in the fall, trapped in the winter and took to the river in the summer.

During the previous year Carmack had taught Jim and Charley how to pan for gold. Now they had caught Carmack's excitement about making a prospecting trip down to the Stewart River country, but they all realized they had neither the supplies nor the money to outfit for such an extended trip. They decided to work another season packing for others out of Dyea. Strong-minded Kate insisted on going with them.

The Carmack group was fortunate to get a big packing job almost immediately after arriving at Dyea in May 1887.

A Canadian surveyor named William Ogilvie had been dispatched by the Dominion government to survey from salt water at Dyea over the Chilkoot Pass to the chain of lakes in the upper Yukon country. His equipment and a two-year supply of food were piled up on the beach at Dyea. Ogilvie hired 120 packers, all Chilkoots except the Carmack party of four, to move his outfit to Lake Bennett.

While the packers were at work on the trail, Ogilvie busied himself with the survey and supervised another project. The cliff-like approach to the Chilkoot Pass precluded a wagon road or railroad on that route to the upper Yukon valley. At Juneau, Ogilvie had heard stories about another route through the coastal mountains, roughly paralleling the Chilkoot Trail, beginning at the mouth of another coastal river, some four miles southeast of Dyea, and he asked Captain William Moore, accompanied by Skookum Jim, to undertake a reconnaissance survey of the route. With no trail, thick brush and swollen streams, the trip required a week of hard travel. Captain Moore reported that the new route was superior to the Chilkoot Trail as a possible roadway into the Yukon country in the distant future. The Indians called the pass at the summit of the new route Shasheki, but Ogilvie gave it a new name: White Pass, after the Honourable Thomas White, Canada's Minister of the Interior.

Meanwhile, there was trouble at the Chilkoot Pass. The Chilkoot packers refused to go beyond the summit, apparently fearful of belligerent tribes in the interior. After being paid off they returned to Dyea, leaving the Ogilvie party stranded at the summit. Carmack came to the rescue. He returned to Dyea and recruited nine Tagish packers to get the expedition moving again. The job took six weeks.

When the season ended in the fall of 1887, Skookum Jim, Tagish Charley and Carmack planned a long prospecting trip down the Yukon the following summer. His Tagish friends helped Carmack build a ten- by 12-foot log cabin at Dyea, where he would winter. In the spring, when Jim and Charley brought their winter catch of furs to Healy's trading post at Dyea, Carmack would rejoin them for the return to Tagish and beyond.

Carmack had been in love with Kate for months. Although he had lived in the same house with her at Tagish and traveled with her on the Chilkoot Trail, he had never slept with her. Now, he wanted her to stay with him at Dyea; that was why he had built the cabin.

Kate had spent the summer packing to be near Carmack. Here at Dyea, away from the influence of her mother, an independent girl could do as she pleased. When Carmack, speaking in Tagish, asked Kate whether she wanted to spend the winter with him, she smiled and said yes. Carmack put his arms around her and kissed her for the first time.

Kate moved into their crude log cabin. When night came they spread their bearskin sleeping robes on the dirt floor and blew out the candle. No native or civil or religious marriage ceremony was ever performed; they just began living together. What started out as a temporary arrangement gradually grew into a more-or-less permanent relationship, a common-law marriage that was to haunt Carmack years later.

Chapter 5

Roaming the Yukon

One sunny afternoon in May 1888, while Kate was hanging her flour-sack panties on the clothesline outside the Carmack cabin at Dyea, she caught sight of two men scurrying down the Taiya River trail. The husky one, swinging his massive head from side to side and carrying a big load of furs on his back, she recognized as her brother Jim. The slender one wearing a red neckerchief must be her nephew Charley.

Waving her arms and shouting effusive greetings, she sprinted up the trail to meet her relatives. George Carmack, suddenly awakened from his nap, followed her in his stocking feet. Kate showered Jim and Charley with rapid-fire questions in her native Tagish. After a winter in the cabin while Carmack worked on repairs around the trading post, she was anxious for news. How was her sister Jennie? How were Charley's brothers and his sister? How were all the others at the Tagish village?

Kate chattered away so incessantly that half an hour went by before Carmack was able to show his partners the supplies he had gathered for their prospecting trip down the Yukon.

The next day Skookum Jim and Tagish Charley sold their furs, mostly muskrat and mink pelts, with a few beaver and fox, at the Healy & Wilson Trading Post. Carmack watched as the two men purchased a year's supply of tobacco, ammunition and other necessities.

"We're leaving for the Yukon in the morning," Carmack told Healy.

"When you coming back?" asked the trader.

Carmack finished lighting his pipe before he replied.

"When we make the big find and strike it rich."

Healy shook his head. Carmack saw a look that said "I've heard that before."

Aware of Carmack's fondness for sweets, Mrs. Healy presented him with a jar of her homemade currant jelly.

In the morning, Carmack and his three companions hoisted bulky packs on their backs and started up the long climb to the Chilkoot Pass and the lakes beyond. A week later the travelers reached the Tagish village, where they received a boisterous welcome from relatives and friends. Kate had expected to accompany her man on the prospecting trip but Carmack had decided otherwise. When the three men loaded their boat and pushed off, Kate was left behind, kicking and screaming.

The trio paddled down the chain of lakes that empties into the Yukon, that majestic sub-Arctic river highway into the Canadian wilderness. They wasted no time prospecting on the rivers and creeks that Carmack had explored during his 1885 trip but continued downstream until they reached the mouth of the Hootalinqua (now the Teslin) River, where they began panning.

Carmack knew that the Mother Lode district of California was part of the Rocky Mountains. He also knew that the gold diggings in Nevada, Colorado and British Columbia were in the same mountain system. Because the Rocky Mountain range extends northward through Canada and Alaska, Carmack believed that similar deposits of gold would someday be discovered in the mountainous regions of the Yukon basin.

Millions of years ago, when the Rocky Mountains began their upward thrust, scattered veins of gold in quartz and other hard-rock formations were exposed by erosion. Streams transported small pieces of angular, sharp-edged lode gold down the mountainsides. As the pieces tumbled downhill, they gradually became rounded and smooth. Finally, the gold came to rest on the streambanks, in the form of dust or nuggets. These accumulations of sand and gravel containing water-worn gold are known as placer deposits.

Recovering gold that remains locked in bedrock in lode deposits is a time-consuming and costly operation requiring large expenditures of money. The gold-bearing rocks must be blasted loose and crushed in stamp mills; the powdery residue must be subjected to chemical processes to free the gold.

Gold in a placer mine—often called the poor man's mine—may be quickly and inexpensively recovered, however, by washing the gold-bearing sands in sluice boxes or rockers. The sluice box was a long, inclined trough with riffle-bars in the bottom. The miner would shovel in the gold-bearing dirt, then wash it down with water. The sand and gravel would wash out, leaving the heavy gold behind, caught in the riffles. Rocker boxes used a rocking action to wash out the gravel and rocks.

By panning the sand at carefully selected spots, Carmack and his partners were trying to locate such easily mined patches. They panned samples from around boulders in the stream bed or wherever streaks of black magnetite sand were found on the river bars.

"Here, looky here, behind that rock," Carmack would say to Jim, who would scoop up a shovelful of sand and toss it into the pan. Wearing rubber boots and standing ankle-deep in the stream, Carmack would fill the pan with water and wash away the floating bits of leaves, bark and other organic material. He picked out the larger pieces of gravel, then rocked the pan back and forth with a swishing motion, occasionally tilting the pan forward to permit the lighter material to escape. Gradually, the coarser sand washed away until only a residue of fine black sand remained. If no streaks of bright color appeared in the pan, the residue was thrown away and another sample taken elsewhere.

Whenever shining particles of gold appeared, Carmack picked out the larger specks with tweezers. The remainder of the black sand he placed in a small bottle. Later, he would dry the residue, then pour it into a small, wedge-shaped brass blower pan; then he could blow away the lighter black sand, leaving the fine gold behind.

After a month of persistent probing with pick and pan along the streams that emptied into the lower Hootalinqua, Carmack and his partners took stock of their findings. They had found only a few ounces of flour gold and a dozen flakes the size of a pinhead, but nothing large enough to be described as coarse gold.

"Well, fellows, it's plain as a moose track in snow," Carmack told his companions. "We ain't never going to make a strike 'round here. Let's pack up and move on."

The three men drifted down the Yukon to the mouth of the Big Salmon River before resuming their panning. They were now about 175 miles downstream from the Tagish village. Working both sides of the Big Salmon, they tested dozens of sandbars.

They found colors almost everywhere—flour gold in many spots—but very little coarse gold, nothing larger than a grain of wheat. By mid-August Carmack estimated their total take of gold for the season was close to ten ounces, worth about $160. Disappointed but not disheartened, the three men began the journey upstream to the Tagish village.

During their first season of full-time searching for gold, Skookum Jim and Tagish Charley had picked up a good working knowledge of the uncertain craft of prospecting. Charley, who could expertly wash down a panful of dirt or sand in less than two minutes, proved to be faster than either Jim or Carmack. However, Jim seemed to have a natural talent for the finer nuances of prospecting, showing better judgement than Charley in selecting spots where gold was likely to be found. Both had succumbed to gold fever; already they were discussing plans for another season of prospecting farther down the Yukon.

Despite the hardships and disappointments of the summer, Carmack was pleased with his second venture into the Yukon. The daily joy of life on the river more than made up for the dashed hopes found in the pan. Also, he had improved his prospecting techniques. For one thing, he had come to realize that the methods used to locate profitable placer deposits in California could not always be applied to the Yukon region.

Along the relatively short rivers on the slopes of the Sierra Nevada Mountains in California, coarse gold frequently appeared along the river bars. In the Yukon country, only flour gold was found in the sandbars along the major rivers. Because the gold had been transported for greater distances down much longer rivers, the gold particles had been worn down to a finer size. Carmack resolved that on his next prospecting trip he would concentrate his search for nuggets and coarse gold along the creeks and smaller streams.

By the time Carmack and his partners reached the Tagish village, the frosts of early September were sparkling the grass each morning. Jim settled back into the big community house while Charley joined his brothers and sister in their separate dwelling. Kate and Carmack moved into an old cabin.

While Carmack patched up the leaky sod roof, Kate rechinked the logs with moss and clay to keep out the winter cold and summer mosquitoes. She was happy to have her man back. She was also the envy of other Tagish women, who considered it a great honor to be sleeping with a white man. Pleased with the cheerful way she looked after his needs, the easy-going Carmack did not allow her moody disposition or her occasional outbursts of temper to disturb him.

In autumn Carmack once again joined the Tagish men hunting for moose and caribou. The Indians were dependent upon the white man for their tea, tobacco and ammunition; everything else they needed came from the forest, the lakes or the streams. In addition to hunting the larger game animals, they also snared rabbits, squirrels and porcupines. Ducks and geese were shot in the fall. Trout, salmon and whitefish were caught in great quantities and dried for use when winter cold sealed the lakes and river. In the spring, a few edible roots became available, and summer brought blueberries and salmonberries. When the villagers ran out of tea, spruce or willow tea took its place.

To go with the frying-pan bread that Carmack liked so well, Kate made bone butter. After the caribou bones had been fleshed and dried for a day or two, Kate pounded them into a pulp with a rock. The crushed bones were simmered for several hours, and then the liquid strained through a cloth and set aside to cool. The fatty marrow was skimmed off, simmered again, then allowed to cool and gel. The resulting bone butter came out white as freshly fallen snow.

Carmack, the only blue-eyed man in the village, once again fell easily into Tagish ways. He became accustomed to doing without the many foods that prospectors considered essential: sugar, dried fruit, canned vegetables and that old standby, bacon and beans. His knowledge of the Tagish language grew daily until he was perfectly at ease talking with the villagers. During the long winter nights there was plenty of time for conversations with Jim and Charley, making plans for their next prospecting trip.

In spite of socializing with the Tagish, there was one thing Carmack missed very much: his family back in California. He had not heard from Rose since he left Dyea. On Christmas Eve 1888, a nostalgic Carmack wrote a poem in his pocket diary.

Christmas Thoughts
I am camped on a mountainside tonight,
A hundred miles from the sea,
And the smell of caribou steak on the coals
Is a grateful odor to me.

For the deer were fleet-footed and shy today,
And I've roamed the mountain's breast,
Till the bear-skin robe on my cosy bed,
Seems beckoning me to rest.

But a tall old spruce by the campfire's glow
Bows its glittering top to me,
And seems to whisper, "It's Christmas Eve
And I'm your Christmas tree."

Then a flood of memories o'er me creep,
And my spirit afar doth roam,
To where there's another glittering tree,
In a California home.

There all is light and life and love,
And the children laugh with glee,
And I cannot but wonder with wistful pain,
Are they thinking tonight of me?

But a whispering comes from the tall old spruce,
And my soul from pain is free,
For I know when they kneel together tonight,
They'll all be praying for me.[1]

Late in May of 1889, after the ice on Lake Tagish had broken up into giant, jagged, blue chunks and moved noisily northward into Lake Marsh, small boats filled with prospectors began to drift past the Tagish village. Hungry for news of any sort, Carmack climbed on a beach boulder, shouting and waving at one of the boats. The four occupants paddled toward shore. They were on their way to Fortymile, a mining camp about 500 miles downstream from Tagish.

Coarse gold, lots of it, had been discovered in the Fortymile region in the fall of 1886, they told Carmack. As he listened to their tales of the richness and wide extent of the new gold fields, Carmack tingled with excitement. Plenty of unstaked placer ground remained, they assured him. That settled it; Carmack and his Tagish prospecting buddies would start for the new diggings at once.

While Skookum Jim and Tagish Charley were eager to go prospecting again, they were not prepared for an immediate start. They wanted to make a trip to the trading post at Dyea to sell their furs and buy more tobacco, ammunition and prospecting supplies.

Another more serious complication also had to be considered. Once they were at Fortymile, they would have to winter there. It would be impossible to get back to the Tagish village before the fall freeze-up.

Determined to be back for the autumn hunts and winter trapping, Jim and Charley decided not to make the journey to Fortymile with Carmack. Instead, after their return from Dyea, the two Tagish men would strike out on their own for a summer of prospecting somewhere in the upper Yukon valley. They offered to trade their share of the gold obtained during the previous summer for Carmack's winter catch of furs; Carmack agreed. He would use the additional gold to buy supplies when he reached the trading post at Fortymile.

Even after she learned it would mean an absence of a year or more from her village, Kate insisted on making the Fortymile trip with her man. Her dark eyes glowed with excitement as she helped Carmack load their boat.

"So long, Jim! So long, Charley! We'll be back next summer with hiyu gold!" shouted Carmack as he and Kate climbed into the boat and pushed off. Carmack could not foresee that several years would go by before he and Kate would be reunited with her family.

Kate and Carmack arrived at Fortymile in June 1889. The mining settlement was near the junction of the Fortymile River and the Yukon. The camp itself was on Canadian soil but most of the Fortymile gold diggings were on the Alaskan side of the border.

Much to his amazement, Carmack learned that Fortymile gold was found not along the river bars as in other placer diggings near the Yukon, but in dry gulches and benches, many of them located some distance from the nearest stream. The gold-bearing sands of the Fortymile lay deep in the ground. Prospectors were sinking shafts through 20, 30 and even 40 feet of worthless overburden to reach the paydirt found in the cracks and crevices of the bedrock.

Thawing the frozen ground with fires every night, hoisting buckets of slushy muck to the surface every morning, the miners slowly sank their prospect holes toward bedrock. When sampling by panning revealed that a paystreak had been reached, the layer of paydirt was carefully excavated and stored in huge piles called winter dumps, to be sluiced in the spring.

After the floods of spring had freed the creeks of their straitjackets of ice, the gum-booted miners shoveled their paydirt into the trough-like sluice boxes. The lighter bits of sand and soil washed away while the heavier particles of gold sank to the bottom. Then came the payoff for the months of arduous underground work by candlelight in 50° below zero weather: the cleanup—taking in the gold caught by the sluice boxes. After removing the riffle-bars in the bottom of the boxes, the happy miners scooped up the shining gold nuggets and gold dust captured by the bars.

Having hastily examined the Nugget Gulch area where the overburden was rumored to be shallow, Carmack staked out a claim and began digging a shaft in the permanently frozen ground. When Carmack's shaft was six feet deep, he teamed up with a neighboring miner for a two-man dirt-hoisting operation.

Carmack reached bedrock in mid-August. Carefully he spooned the sand and gravel from the larger crevices into his pan. Kate brought him a bucket of water from a nearby creek. Swishing the water around and around, Carmack peered anxiously into the pan. Eventually nothing but black sand remained. No nuggets, no coarse gold, no gold dust. Nothing. He washed out a half dozen more pans of carefully selected samples. The results were the same: nothing. In the risky business of prospecting, Carmack had drawn another blank.

With very little gold left in his poke, Carmack pondered what to do next. It was too late in the season to search out another claim and dig down to bedrock before winter set in. Kate wanted to return to Tagish, but it was too late for that too. Then a neighboring prospector, who had also drawn a blank, told Carmack he was going downriver for a winter of trapping. He suggested Carmack join him, and Carmack accepted. Pulling up the stakes marking the four corners of his claim, he tossed them on the evening campfire.

Carmack and Kate drifted down the Yukon to the mouth of the Porcupine River, below Fort Yukon, and ascended the Porcupine to Rampart House, just inside the Canadian border, where they found a trading post and a small Indian village. Moving into a deserted cabin, they prepared for the winter trapping season.

In the spring, they descended the Porcupine and paddled upstream to Fort Yukon, where Carmack sold his winter catch of furs. They continued upstream to Fortymile. Once again, a hopeful Carmack staked a claim in Nugget Gulch, a four-mile-long ravine ending on the left bank of the Fortymile River.

The Carmacks lived in a tent during the summer of 1890. While George worked hard at the diggings, Kate sewed moccasins and mittens, which she sold to miners. When September came, Carmack was pleased. He had found gold at bedrock. He made plans to stay for the winter, but was too busy sluicing out his paydirt to waste time building a cabin. As the leaves fell and freeze-up came, Kate railed at Carmack for his failure to provide a house for the winter.

Though the winter was long and cold, Carmack remained happy with the paydirt coming out of his claim. Kate, however, was miserable with the cold and discomfort of the tent, which made it almost impossible for her to sew. Yet, for the first time, Carmack began introducing Kate to his friends and neighbors as his wife.

During the 1891 spring cleanup, Carmack's claim yielded a substantial amount of coarse gold and nuggets. Well-pleased, Carmack built a cabin and prepared for a second year of mining. The cleanup in May 1892 disappointed him, however. He realized the pocket of paydirt he had been working was exhausted.

He decided to abandon his claim and leave the Fortymile country. Kate, who had not seen her brother Jim and other relatives for more than three years, used her sharp tongue to urge him to move closer to the Tagish village.

During his stay in the area, Carmack had observed the thriving business enjoyed by the trading post at Fortymile. Miners made purchases and Yukon valley Indians brought in large amounts of furs. With a fair-sized stake in hand, Carmack decided to open a trading post on the Yukon River a few miles above Five Finger Rapids and only 200 miles from the Tagish village. He purchased a small stock of trading goods, loaded his boat and headed upstream.

At the mouth of the Big Salmon River, he built his trading post of logs, squared by hand, about 18 by 24 feet. The

Indians of the area soon learned about the new establishment and all summer long they drifted in to trade furs for supplies.

That summer of 1892, the wood-burning paddlewheel steamer *Arctic* came up the river to Fort Selkirk with the supplies Carmack had ordered before leaving Fortymile. While transporting his supplies from Selkirk to his post, some 50 miles upriver, Carmack met Reverend T.H. Canham, who planned to establish a mission church for the Church of England. The missionary had brought a supply of lumber, nails, glass and other building materials, but needed help to construct the log church. Carmack agreed to build it, completing the job in the fall of 1892. St. Andrew's Church at Fort Selkirk was the most elaborate structure in the upper Yukon valley, with real glass windows, a belltower, and even a picket fence around the churchyard.

Kate, who was now pregnant, took care of the trading post while Carmack worked for the missionary. When her time drew near, Carmack closed the post for the winter and moved her into the settlement at Fort Selkirk.

On January 11, 1893, a daughter was born to Kate and George Carmack. Kate gave the baby a Tagish name, Ahgay, meaning "daughter of the lake". Unable to pronounce the child's Tagish name to Kate's satisfaction, Carmack named his daughter Graphie Grace, after a character in a book he had borrowed from Canham's library. Canham christened the baby Graphie Grace Carmack.

While Kate cared for their infant daughter, Carmack fed the fire, prepared the meals, and also attended to another little chore. As Indian mothers had been doing for countless years, Kate used moss as diapers and it was George's task to see that there was always a good supply on hand.

In the spring, Carmack took his wife and daughter back to the trading post above Five Finger Rapids. He continued operating there, and mining the seam of coal he had found, until the spring of 1896, when dwindling trade and profits forced him to abandon both enterprises.

In May of 1896, Carmack moved his family downriver to Fortymile, where he settled his account with the local trader and began wondering what he should do next.

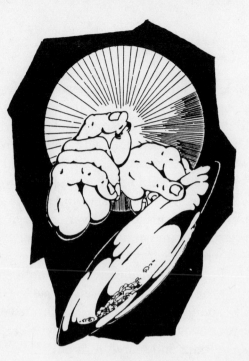

Chapter 6

Carmack Discovers Klondike Gold

One June night in 1896, while George Carmack was sleeping in his tent at Fortymile, he experienced a dream so real, so vivid and so exciting that further sleep was impossible. He dreamed he was sitting on the bank of a small stream looking at a school of grayling surfacing in a pool of blue-green water. Suddenly the sail-like dorsal fins of the grayling disappeared and two large king salmon swam into the pool. Their scales were made of shiny flakes of gold, and gold pieces covered their eyes. When he reached down to grab a golden salmon, Carmack awoke to find himself clutching his right ear.[1]

The golden scales and eyes suggested to Carmack that somewhere, in close association with salmon in a stream with blue-green water, there was gold, big chunks of gold, waiting for him. Where could such a stream be found? The brownish Yukon was heavy with silt, and many of its tributaries were milky or muddy. However, emptying into the Yukon 55 miles upstream from Fortymile was a well-known salmon stream whose clear waters turned blue-green under summer skies. Prospectors called it the Klondike, an Anglicized version of the Indian name used by natives of the Yukon valley. Responding to a powerful intuitive impulse, Carmack decided to start for the Klondike River, where he would fish for salmon and search for gold.

Before leaving Fortymile, Carmack bought some net-twine at Jack McQuesten's trading post, and Kate helped him make a long gill-net suitable for catching king salmon. On July first, the couple loaded their boat and started upstream, accompanied by a prospector friend, Lou Cooper, who had staked a hard-rock claim on the Yukon opposite the mouth of the Klondike. Three-year-old Graphie sat on a pile of netting while the adults took turns poling the boat upstream.

At the mouth of the Klondike River, Carmack pitched his tent on the beach and made camp. The Klondike was low and clear, with a delicate blue-green tint, just the way he had seen it in his dream. Several families of Yukon Indians had fish camps in the vicinity. Awaiting the annual run of king salmon, Carmack built an Indian-style fish weir of willow poles in the Klondike, and set out his long gill-net in the Yukon.

The usual heavy summer runs of king salmon failed to appear that year, and Carmack's nets remained empty most of the time. Some of the Indians blamed the lack of fish on the steamboats downriver, saying the paddlewheels churning the water made the salmon turn back.

After three weeks of unproductive work, Carmack realized that he would not be able to put up enough dried fish to feed his family during the coming winter. Even the weather turned against him. Heavy rains fell during the last week of July, followed by a spell of cold weather that froze the heavy morning dew into droplets of ice.

Late in July, as Carmack was picking a salmon out of his gill-net, he saw a small boat manned by his old friends, sturdy, broad-backed Skookum Jim and wiry Tagish Charley, now sporting a wispy mustache.

Not until he shook hands did Carmack recognize the third member of the group. Ten years before, while wintering at Tagish, he had taught a few words of English to Kulsin, Tagish Charley's youngest brother. The boy wanted a white man's name, so Carmack had given him one: Patsy Henderson. Now, at 17, Patsy was taller than his older brother.

Kate Carmack, happy to see her brother Jim again, proudly showed off her daughter, Graphie. Jim announced that he had married a Chilkoot Indian girl and that a daughter, Daisy, had been born to them the previous summer. His wife and daughter were at the Tagish village, awaiting his return. In spurts of loud and rapid Tagish, Kate asked Jim for news of her relatives and learned that shortly after she had left home, her sister followed Kate's example and went off with a prospector named Wilson. Their daughter Mary was now five years old. Jim had received no news of them for more than two years. Tagish Charley had also married and had a daughter named Susy.

The campfire burned late that night as the three men recounted their respective experiences since they had gone their separate ways. Jim rolled up his sleeves and pointed to the scars on his arms, the result of a face-to-face encounter with a big brown bear. Spotting the brownie on the beach near Dyea, he had gone after him. The bear spotted Jim, growled and charged. Jim fired his rifle. The bear kept coming. Jim emptied his rifle, then shoved the barrel down the bear's throat. After making several swipes at Jim, the wounded bear suddenly collapsed and rolled over on its back. Jim had hoisted a rock the size of a water bucket, and dropped it on the bear's head, ending the fight.

Although Jim and Charley had occasionally prospected for gold after Carmack left them, they found nothing more than a rare flash of colors in the pan. Their fall hunts for caribou were disappointing and even catches from the winter traplines had fallen off. Bad luck seemed to have followed them ever since Carmack's departure, so they consulted the shaman at Tagish. He advised them to rejoin their old prospecting companion if they wished to be rid of the evil spirits.

When Carmack told his friends about his dream of golden salmon swimming in blue-green water, they were easily persuaded to join him on a prospecting trip up the Klondike valley. Jim wanted to start out the next morning.

"I'm anxious to start up the Klondike," Carmack said. "That's why I came here. But first, I want to lay in a good supply of salmon for the winter. After the salmon come, then we'll go prospecting."

"Maybe salmon no come. You got chickamin buy grub?"

"I got no chickamin," Carmack said, shaking his head. "If the fish don't come, we'll do something to get chickamin. Listen. On your way down here, did you see Joe Ladue's sawmill at Ogilvie?"

"Yes."

"There's another sawmill at Fortymile. They buy logs.

We'll cut down some big trees, raft the logs down to Fortymile. We sell logs, buy grub, go prospecting."

"No big trees this place."

"Listen. Lou Cooper has a quartz claim over there," Carmack said, pointing to the opposite side of the Yukon. "Lou says there are lots of big spruce trees up the Klondike. That's where we'll get logs and that's where we'll start prospecting."

"When do we get logs?"

"After the salmon run is over."

A few evenings later, just after Carmack and his companions had finished their supper, a small, heavily loaded boat with a single occupant pulled up to the beach. Carmack recognized the tall, slender man with the half-moon mustache as Bob Henderson, a prospector. They had met at Carmack's trading post in 1894, when Henderson boated down the Yukon for the first time. When Carmack walked down the beach to meet the visitor, Jim and Charley followed.

"Hello, Bob," Carmack said, speaking in his usual slow, deliberate manner. "I heard at Fortymile that you were working for Billy Redford up on Quartz Creek. You still there?"

"No, George. I left Redford a long time ago. Went over the divide to a little creek on the other side of the Dome. I've got a good prospect going there—named the creek Gold Bottom."

"Where you headed for now?"

"Back to Gold Bottom. I've been up to Joe Ladue's trading post at Ogilvie. Came down from Gold Bottom by way of the Indian River, but the water there is so low I can't go back that way. I'll have to take the long way around, to where Gold Bottom empties into the Klondike."

"Is your prospect any good?"

Henderson shrugged. "I've got three fellows working with me and when we get down to bedrock I'll know just how good it is."

"Any chance for us to stake up there?" asked Carmack.

Henderson looked at Jim and Charley before replying.

"There is for you, George. But I don't want any damn Siwashes staking on Gold Bottom."

Carmack's blue eyes widened in disbelief at the callousness of Henderson's remark. Jim's dark face flushed. He clenched his hands as he glared at Henderson. Charley curled his lip and kicked at the beach sand. After a long tense silence, Henderson pushed his boat into the water and started up the Klondike. In the days ahead he would have reason to regret his bigotry.

"What's matta dat white man?" asked Jim as the three men walked back to their camp. "Him killet Inchen moose, Inchen caribou, ketchet gold Inchen country, no liket Inchen stake claim, what for, no good."

"Never mind," Carmack said. "We'll find a creek of our own, and we'll all stake on it, you and me and Charley. Listen. I think the salmon run is about over. Let's go up the Klondike tomorrow and start looking around for big trees."

Leaving Kate behind to take care of Graphie and the gill-net, Jim, Charley, Patsy and Carmack started up the Klondike valley. About five miles upstream they found the first of several stands of spruce trees big enough for saw logs.

On their first day of logging, the four men felled and trimmed five trees, then struggled to roll the heavy logs through tangled underbrush to the water. Carmack realized how impossible his logging venture would have been without the help of his Tagish friends. By the second day they were cutting down only trees within a tree-length of the river, and the work went faster. Ten days later, Carmack took out his measuring tape and scaled 50 logs they had cut.

At $25 per thousand board feet, the wood would sell for about $200, enough to pay for a sizable supply of food for the winter.

"Now we prospect?"

"Tomorrow," Carmack said, smiling at Jim's impatience. "We'll prospect every creek we run across." What he did not tell Jim was that he planned to strike out for the Dome, the highest mountain in the area, and look for Henderson's camp.

After an early breakfast, Carmack peeked at his sleeping daughter, and leaned over to kiss her. One of the first words Graphie had learned to say was "Pot," a word that soon became her father's pet name for her.

"Don't let little Pot play near the river," he told Kate. "We'll be back in a week or so. Then we'll take the logs downriver and get some grub."

Carmack, Jim and Charley loaded their prospecting equipment and supplies into their boat and began poling the boat up the Klondike. Patsy remained at the fish camp with Kate to look after the gill-net.

The prospectors had traveled upstream only a few miles when they came to a quiet backwater slough, where they pulled the boat out of the water. With Carmack in the lead, they set off through the woods, each man carrying a light pack, Jim armed with the same rifle he had used in his battle with the big brownie. After thrashing around in the dew-laden underbrush for an hour, they came out of the timber to a small creek.

Directly in front of them was a gravel bar sprinkled with tiny pieces of white quartz. Carmack slipped off his pack and reached for his gold pan. He filled the pan with fine gravel and sand taken from the upper part of the bar. Swishing water back and forth, he panned down to a fistful of sand.

Charley rushed over to look.

"What for you talket dat cultus wawa? I no seeum gold."

"Charley, I'm making Boston man's medicine. Spit in the pan for good luck; you too, Jim."

Both men complied. Carmack continued panning until only a spoonful of black sand remained in the pan. He scooped up a little more water, gently swirling it around until a streak of bright yellow gold appeared. The gold dust was fine but heavy, easy to save in the pan. Carmack wondered what kind of showing he would get if he could find exposed bedrock farther up the creek.

Once again the three men hoisted their packs and continued their hike up the creek valley. After traveling for more than an hour, they sat down to rest on top of a steep bank. Digging into the bank near its base, Carmack uncovered a pocket of soft, crumbling rock. He tossed a shovelful into his pan and quickly panned it down. In the residue, he found a good showing of fine gold and two pieces of coarse gold about the size of grains of rice.

"Hey, looky here," Carmack said. "Coarse gold."

"Now we stake," declared Jim.

Carmack shook his head.

"We don't know what's upstream yet. Let's keep going and looking for bedrock in the creek. If we don't find anything better, we can always come back here."

Jim and Charley agreed and they tramped on for another hour or so before making camp.

The next morning Carmack and his partners continued working their way up the creek, panning here and there, getting a little flour gold in nearly every pan, but no coarse gold. Coming to a fork in the creek, they paused briefly before deciding to follow the larger branch. The stream they passed over, later named Eldorado Creek, would turn out to be the richest gold-bearing creek in the Yukon.

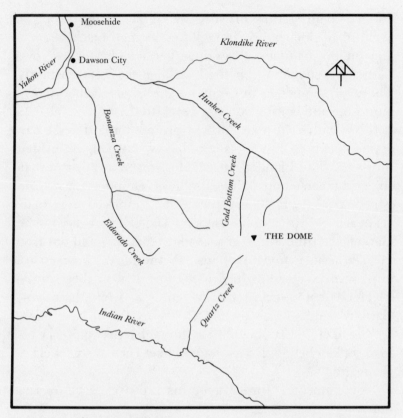

Klondike region of the Yukon.

A little farther upstream, they came to a pile of rotting, half-burned logs, the remains of an old campfire. Although Carmack was not aware of it at the time, Joe Ladue had camped on this spot while hunting moose many years before.

Following the dim trails made by wandering game, the three prospectors followed the creek to its source, then climbed to the top of a ridge to look around. Carmack pointed to a bald, round-topped mountain known as the Dome. They headed toward it, pushing their way through heavy underbrush and thickets of thorny devil's club that stabbed them as they brushed by. While going through a patch of huckleberries, Jim spotted a small black bear sitting on his haunches. Leveling his Winchester .44 over Carmack's shoulder, he fired, killing the bear instantly. The men skinned it out, cut up the meat, cached it in a birch tree and continued their climb to the top.

It was worth the hike. A rocky promontory offered a panoramic view of broad valleys below, bathed in brilliant sunshine. The blended colors of crimson and purple and emerald green along the creek valleys reminded Carmack of a fancy tapestry he had seen in a San Francisco store many years ago. A fringe of huckleberry and salmonberry bushes marked the timberline on the ridges that fingered out from the Dome in many directions. To the north, a wispy column of blue smoke drifted upward from a small canyon.

"Henderson's camp. Let's go see what he's got," Carmack said.

"No liket," said Jim. "What for tellet that cultus white man we ketchet gold? Dis man no liket Inchen staket claim. We no go."

"Aw, come on, Jim. Maybe his prospect is better than ours."

After a little more coaxing, Jim agreed to go. The three men descended the brushy canyon leading to Henderson's camp.

"Hello, George," Henderson said. "You found us, eh?"

"Well, yes, although it was accidental. We found a good prospect on a creek over on the other side of the Dome. Saw your camp from the Dome, so we decided to come down here and tell you about it."

Henderson took Carmack to the open cut where Frank Swanson, Al Dalton and Charley Monson, Henderson's partners, were digging down to bedrock. Carmack asked for permission to try a few pans; Henderson assented. Panning samples taken from both the open cut and along the edge of Gold Bottom Creek, Carmack found only a modest showing of colors in the pan. At Henderson's insistence, Carmack staked a claim downstream from Henderson's, but he declined to stay and work it.

"Bob, take a look at what I found on that creek of ours," Carmack said, displaying the two bits of gold he was carrying in an empty cartridge. "You better come have a look."

Henderson shook his head.

"I'm staying here until we get down to bedrock."

"Suit yourself. You recorded yet?"

"Hell, no. That can wait."

Carmack and his two partners were almost out of tobacco. Noticing that Henderson had an ample supply, Jim tried to buy some, but Henderson curtly refused him. When Jim began mumbling in Tagish, Carmack put an end to further conversation.

"Well, we'd better start back. We got a long ways to go."

According to Carmack's estimate, Henderson's camp was about 15 miles from the spot where the trio had found gold—30 miles above their fish camp at the mouth of the Klondike.

Camping overnight as they went, the Carmack party followed Gold Bottom Creek up to its head on the Dome, then took a shortcut that passed through a swampy area. Mosquitoes and gnats pestered them, and mud sucked at their heels as they struggled to keep their footing in the swamp. After reaching the ridges again, following their previous trail, they found their bear-meat cache without difficulty. Then they followed the ridge-top route until they caught sight of their creek, the one where they had found the bits of coarse gold. They followed the creek down to the fork they had bypassed earlier.

Carmack walked up Eldorado Creek and tried a few pans.

He found ruby and black sand in the pan, nothing more. The three worked their way downstream from the fork, staying close to the creek and panning frequently. Now, fine gold was showing up in every pan. About half a mile below the fork, the creek made a sharp turn to the north, and the men climbed the steep bank ahead of them. Carmack looked down at the creek, 50 feet away. A long, narrow strip of black bedrock showed along its bed.

"Bedrock," he shouted. "If this creek is any good at all, we'll find gold down there."

Carmack slipped off his pack and scrambled down the bank to the creek. There was something shiny in the shallow water flowing over the rim of the bedrock. He reached down and picked up a gold nugget the size and shape of a wrinkled dime. Placing the nugget between his teeth, he bit it. The nugget bent, and stayed bent. Gold! Carmack held the nugget high in the air and shouted to his companions on the bank.

"Hiyu gold! Bring pan and shovel. Hurry!"

Charley grabbed the pan and shovel, sliding down the bank so fast that he tripped and fell. Carmack caught him before he rolled into the water. Turning over a flat piece of rock with the shovel, Carmack saw flakes of gold lodged in the crevice. He scooped up a shovelful of crumbling bedrock and tossed it into the pan. Quickly he washed it down. It produced at least a quarter of an ounce of flaky coarse gold.

"A five-dollar pan," yelled Carmack. "We've hit it—the golden paystreak!"

Jim stared at the gold. He scooped it up in his hand, then let it dribble through his fingers back into the pan. Charley stared too, slack-jawed with wonder. Carmack felt the blood pounding through his temples. Elation surged through him, overwhelming him. He threw the pan to the ground and leaped high in the air. Then he began dancing around the pan, a dance remotely related to a Scottish hornpipe, an Irish jig, and an Indian version of the hula-hula. Jim and Charley joined him, doing their own interpretations of a Tagish ceremonial dance.

Later, after Carmack washed out a few more pans and obtained enough gold to half-fill a spent shotgun shell in which he had carried matches, the happy prospectors crossed the creek and set up camp in a grove of birch trees. For several days, they had been traveling through the tangled underbrush, getting very little rest. Now they were tired and hungry, but exceedingly joyful.

After a supper of bear steaks and tea, the men sat around the campfire smoking their pipes. When the pipes went out, the Indians began chanting songs in Tagish. They sang of feasts and famine together, of hunting for caribou and moose, of journeys together over snow and ice. When the singing ended, they rolled themselves in their sleeping robes and went to sleep.

As the flames of the campfire flickered and went out, Carmack stared at the glowing coals and thought about all his years of wandering up and down the Yukon in search of the elusive gold. Eleven years of privation and hardship, packing over the Chilkoot Pass, eating Indian food and wearing Indian clothing, panning on hundreds of barren river bars. All that was over, now that he had discovered a real bonanza. Bonanza! That's it! That's what he would name this golden stream—Bonanza Creek. His boyhood dream of finding a great gold field was realized. He could see himself walking around the lawn of a beautiful home in California, Kate all dolled up in fancy clothes, waiting for little Pot to come home from school. Nothing but happy days ahead. He yawned contentedly and went to sleep.

Chapter 7

Carmack Stakes
Discovery Claim on Bonanza

In the morning, after hurriedly washing down a skimpy breakfast with black coffee, the three men set about staking their claims. The Dominion Lands Mining Regulations then in effect for the Yukon district of the Northwest Territories permitted any miner more than 18 years of age, citizen or not, to stake a stream placer claim 500 feet long, measured along the general course of the stream. In width, the claim extended from the base of the hill or bench on one side of the stream to the base of the hill or bench on the opposite side.

On the edge of the flat where they were camped stood a small spruce tree about six inches in diameter. Using his hand ax, Carmack whacked off the top of the tree, leaving a five-foot length of spruce slanting up out of the ground. Singing a few verses of "Home Sweet Home" as he squared up the end of the stump, swinging his ax in time with the tune, Carmack also succeeded in getting Jim to turn his habitual scowl upside down. Charley grinned in approval.

With a stubby pencil Carmack wrote on the upstream side of the squared-up spruce.

To whom it may concern:
I do this day, locate and claim by right of discovery, five hundred feet, running upstream from this notice. Located this 17th day of August, 1896.
G.W. Carmack.[1]

Using Carmack's 50-foot tape, the men measured off 500 feet upstream from the blazed spruce, marking the limit of Carmack's Discovery Claim and the beginning of No. 1 Above, which was staked for Skookum Jim. In similar fashion, No. 1 Below was marked off and claimed by Carmack, who, as discoverer, was entitled to have two claims. No. 2 Below was staked and claimed by Tagish Charley. The Indians could not read or write English, or even read the numbers on the tape, so Carmack did all the marking required to fulfill the legal requirements for staking a claim.

Going back to a tall birch tree near the point of discovery, Carmack peeled off a piece of bark and penciled these words: "I name this creek Bonanza. George Carmack."[2] After the birchbark notice had been attached to the discovery stake with willow twigs, Carmack placed his shovel and gold pan at the base of the stake.

When Carmack was satisfied that all four claims were

Stake marking Discovery Claim on Bonanza Creek. (COURTESY
YUKON ARCHIVES, WHITEHORSE)

properly marked, the three men packed up and started back
to their fish camp at the mouth of the Klondike. Tagish
Charley wanted to stay and begin mining operations at once
with pan and shovel, but Carmack talked him out of that.
One man shoveling dirt into a sluice box, Carmack pointed
out, could handle 20 times as much paydirt as he could by
panning. To build sluice boxes, they needed saws, ham-

mers and nails, all of which they lacked. To get money to purchase the tools and supplies they needed, the logs they had already cut must now be rafted down the Yukon and sold to the sawmill at Fortymile. Only after these operations had been completed, and the sluice boxes built, could the extraction of gold begin in earnest.

After Carmack explained all this, Jim and Charley readily agreed. Carmack began to realize that from now on, in addition to managing his own affairs, he would also have to look after the business concerns of his two partners.

None of them considered backtracking up to Henderson's camp to tell him about their latest find on Bonanza. After all, Carmack had already shown Henderson the coarse gold from their first few pans along Bonanza. Carmack had declared his intention of staking this creek and had invited Henderson to look at the new discovery. Henderson had declined, saying he would stay with the Gold Bottom claim until bedrock was reached. With so much work to be done before the fall freeze-up, Carmack could not afford to waste two days of travel just to tell Henderson something he already knew. Since Henderson had bluntly stated that he did not want Indians staking on Gold Bottom, Jim and Charley naturally did not want Henderson to stake on Bonanza.

Five hours of hard travel brought Carmack and his companions back to the slough where they had secured their boat. While floating down the Klondike, they met four men wading upsteam, pulling a loaded boat. After the usual greetings, the men exchanged names. The newcomers were Dan McGillivery, Dave Edwards, Harry Waugh and Dave McKay.

"Where you fellows heading?" Carmack asked.

"We've just come from Ogilvie," McGillivery said. "Joe Ladue told us that Bob Henderson had found a good prospect on Gold Bottom Creek, so we decided to have a look-see. You know anything about it?"

"Yes, we left there three days ago," Carmack said.

"What do you think of it?"

"Well, I don't like to be a knocker," said Carmack with his irrepressible grin. "But I don't think much of his prospect. Henderson hasn't found anything but flour gold."

McGillivery's tanned and bearded jaw dropped before he replied.

"Then you wouldn't advise us to go up there?"

"No, because I've got something better for you."

After displaying the coarse gold he had found, Carmack gave McGillivery and his companions full directions for reaching his Discovery Claim. Noticing that the McGillivery party had a whip-saw in their boat, Carmack asked if he might borrow it in a couple of days.

"After the tip you gave us, George, you can have the saw any old time you want it," said Dave McKay, who would later stake No. 3 Below Discovery. The other members of the McGillivery party would stake downstream a bit, claiming Nos. 15, 16 and 17 Below Discovery.

The two boats separated and the Carmack group continued their drift down the Klondike. On arrival at the fish camp, Jim and Charley began unloading the boat while George broke the news to Kate.

"Looky here, Kate, looky here!" he yelled.

When he emptied the shotgun shell of coarse gold into her hand, her dark widened and she screamed out her delight in Tagish phrases, then switched to Chinook.

"Hiyu pil chikamin! Hiyu pil chikamin!"

"Yes, Kate, plenty gold, plenty gold."

Charley's brother Patsy came running to see and hold the gold.

"You staket claim for me?"

"No, Patsy, you're too young to stake a claim. Don't worry, I'll see that you get hiyu gold."

Soon after arriving, Carmack hailed two men drifting downstream in a small boat. They were French-Canadians who introduced themselves as Alphonso LePierre and George Remillard.

"Where you boys headed for?" Carmack asked.

"Down the river to Fortymile."

"Don't go any farther. You hear about the new strike?"

"Oh yes, we hear about Bob Henderson from Joe Ladue. I think he is one big bluff," LePierre said.

"How's this for bluff?" asked Carmack, showing them the gold.

Once again Carmack told the story of his discovery on Bonanza Creek and explained how to get there. Soon the two French-Canadians raced across the beach on their way to Bonanza. In their excitement they forgot to tie up their boat, which would have drifted away had Carmack not secured it. The next day Remillard and LePierre staked Nos. 11 and 12 Below Discovery.

Prospecting across the broad Yukon from Carmack's fish camp was Lou Cooper, who had helped Carmack pole his boat upriver from Fortymile only a few weeks before. After supper on discovery day, Carmack rowed across the Yukon to tell his friend his news. Cooper and his partner, Ed Monahan, arrived on Bonanza the next day and staked Nos. 32 and 29 Below Discovery.

On the morning of August 18, Carmack organized his own party.

"Jim, take your tent and set up camp on Discovery Claim. Bring your rifle along and run off any claim-jumpers. Take the ax along and start cutting down trees for building a saw pit. When the rest of us get back from Fortymile, we'll borrow McGillivery's whip-saw and cut up some boards for making sluice boxes. Savvy?"

"Yes."

"Charley, you and Patsy come with me. We're going to take the logs down to the sawmill at Fortymile. It'll take all three of us to handle the raft. If the logs get swept past Fortymile, we're out of luck. Now let's get these logs rafted up."

"Hiyu pil chikamin tenas chuck," Charley said.

"Yes, Charley, there's lots of gold in the creek. But we'll have to move lots of dirt to get it. That'll take time. These logs are as good as money, and right now we need money. We gotta get these logs down to Fortymile. Savvy?"

Charley nodded.

Loaded down with a bulky pack, Skookum Jim waved goodbye with his rifle and started up the trail to Bonanza. Later that morning, after the logs had been rafted into a boom, Carmack and the two brothers climbed into their boat and towed the raft into midstream on the Yukon. In the evening they approached Fortymile, and all hands paddled furiously as they guided the raft up to the sawmill owned by the North American Transportation and Trading Company.

After the delivery was made, Charley and Patsy began setting up camp while Carmack headed for Bill McPhee's saloon, a popular hangout for prospectors and miners.

This was a dramatic occasion and Carmack meant to savor every moment of it, but after two drinks he could no longer restrain himself. He called for quiet before making the announcement of his discovery, realizing many would be moved to action by his story.

By the time Carmack joined Charley and Patsy back at their riverside campsite, half a dozen poling boats were silhouetted in the late evening twilight, heading for the Klondike. By morning every poling boat in Fortymile was gone.

The wild scramble of Fortymile prospectors to reach Carmack's Discovery Claim on Bonanza marked the beginning of a stampede. It continued to gather momentum until, two years later, almost half a million men all over the world had started for the Klondike.

Chapter 8

Winter Mining on Bonanza Creek

After two long days of tiring work poling their boat up the Yukon, George Carmack and his companions, Charley and Patsy, reached their camp at the mouth of the Klondike. Kate and little Graphie ran down the beach to greet them.

"You got needles?" asked Kate in rapid Tagish.

"Sure, I got your needles," Carmack said. "I brought you something else, too."

"What?"

"A can of peaches."

For more than a year, Carmack and his family had eaten

only one fruit: dried apricots, hard as rocks. Kate and Graphie were delighted with the peaches.[1]

The next day was moving day. Everyone except Graphie carried a pack as they broke camp and started out for Discovery Claim, 12 miles away.

Skookum Jim had felled enough trees to build a saw-pit and a few that were suitable for sawing into boards. He had also given in to the temptation to do a little panning. He showed Carmack the two or three ounces of gold dust he had obtained from his own claim, No. 1 Above.

Kate, Graphie and George Carmack set up housekeeping in one tent, while Jim, Charley and Patsy moved into another. Using a whip-saw borrowed from Dave McKay, now one of their neighbors, the four men cut enough boards to build several lengths of sluice boxes. Kate demanded that Carmack start building a cabin for winter shelter, but he refused. The most important consideration right now, he explained, was to wash out as much paydirt as possible before freeze-up put an end to all sluice-box operations.

Within a week after Carmack made his discovery announcement in Bill McPhee's saloon, half a hundred miners had staked claims on Bonanza Creek, and the valley was dotted with tents. Even after Bonanza was staked solid from mouth to source, excited stampeders swarmed into the valley, the late-comers staking on Eldorado Creek, which flowed into Bonanza Creek a short distance above Carmack's discovery.

Carmack had been unable to buy a wheelbarrow in Fortymile so he and his companions began carrying paydirt in sacks and boxes from the exposed bedrock location to their sluice box on the edge of the creek. By mid-September they had washed out 88 ounces of gold for about $1,400.

After all the paydirt from the cracks and crevices of the exposed bedrock had been run through the sluice box, the men began removing the overburden to reach more bedrock. Carmack began sinking a shaft on his claim. Skookum Jim became concerned about the small amount of work being done on his claim.

"When we dig shaft on my claim?" he asked Carmack.

"Listen, Jim, and you too, Charley. We find gold together. Now we have to work together to get gold out. I can't work my two claims by myself. I need your help. You fellows can't work your claims alone either. You need my help. That way everybody helps, no fighting. Jim, Charley, George—three partners. Savvy?"

Jim and Charley nodded. Carmack shook hands with each man. Based on this simple verbal agreement and mutual trust, the three partners would, during the next four years, amicably divide almost a million dollars worth of Klondike gold into three equal shares.

Dominion of Canada mining regulations required that each applicant for a gold placer claim appear in person before an authorized Canadian official and solemnly swear that he had found gold on the claim being recorded. The recording had to be done within 60 days of the initial discovery. Although Carmack was reluctant to interrupt work even briefly, it was important to get the claims properly recorded. So on September 24, 1896, Carmack and his two partners appeared before Acting Commissioner Charles Constantine at Fortymile. Carmack recorded Discovery Claim and No. 1 Below. Skookum Jim, whose name was recorded as Tagish Jim, signed his application for No. 1 Above with an x. Tagish Charley filed for No. 2 Below, also signing with an x.

At Fortymile, Carmack and his partners purchased enough provisions to last through the long Yukon winter. Once again unable to buy wheelbarrows, Carmack bought hardware to build two himself.

Discovery Claim on Bonanza Creek recorded at Fortymile, on September 24, 1896. (COURTESY NORTHWEST COLLECTIONS, UNIVERSITY OF WASHINGTON, SEATTLE)

By the time the Klondike River froze over on October 13, winter mining operations were in full swing on Bonanza Creek. Each evening Carmack or one of his partners would build a fire in the shaft they were sinking and let it burn all night. In the morning, the man in the shaft would shovel the thawed muck into a bucket. Then he would fasten a pig-tail hook at the end of a rope to the bucket, and the man operating the windlass at the top of the shaft would haul the bucket to the surface.

When the bedrock was reached at 14 feet on Discovery Claim, the men started another shaft on Skookum Jim's

George Carmack on Discovery Claim, Bonanza Creek, 1897.
(COURTESY NORTHWEST COLLECTIONS, UNIVERSITY OF
WASHINGTON, SEATTLE)

claim. Most of the work in the shafts had to be done by candlelight; the daylight hours were spent building two log cabins.

After being ice-bound at Fortymile for several days, the river steamer *Arctic* arrived at the mouth of the Klondike on October 17, carrying much-needed supplies and another hundred prospectors.

Joe Ladue, always the enterprising businessman, had staked out a new townsite in September, naming the settlement Dawson City in honor of Canadian geologist George Mercer Dawson. Ladue had dismantled his sawmill at Ogilvie, put it on a raft and floated it down to Dawson City, where he did a good business selling lots and lumber. He also erected the first building in Dawson City, a saloon, which took in more than a hundred ounces of gold every day.

At Kate's urging, Skookum Jim visited the Indian village of Moosehide, only a few miles below Dawson City, returning with a sled-load of furs, which she sewed into mittens to sell to the miners. Sometimes, her enterprise took in more gold in a day than Carmack's. Kate also baked bread for sale, but she refused to do the laundry brought to her by the miners.

A letter that George wrote to his sister Rose and her husband in February indicates that Kate had no need to take in washing.

I thought I would step down and have a little talk with you. I am very well, thank-you and how is yourself? I sent you a letter last fall telling you of the strike I made. Well, it has growed wonderful since then. Everybody here is a millionaire.

Eldorado Creek comes into Bonanza about a half mile above me. It is something wonderful. The pay has been located for four miles now and some of the claims they think will pay a million and not one of them are blanks.

On Bonanza the pay has been located for ten miles and they are all rich. I just struck the pay about a week ago. I have got as high as an ounce and a half to the pan but my paydirt goes about five dollars to the pan. I pan out about $50 a day, besides what goes in the dump.

If I have good luck I will take about four or five thousand to the man this winter and there are four of us working.

I don't know when I will get out of this country. This is only one chance in a lifetime and I must make the best of it. If James were here he would think it was the days of '49 all over again.[2]

Some of the prospectors who had staked on Bonanza or Eldorado creeks had been either careless or overzealous in measuring their 500-foot claim allocations. Squabbles over boundaries were common. Among the late-comers were a few claim-jumpers who pulled up the location stakes put down by others, an act that caused considerable fighting but very little actual bloodshed. Seeking to alleviate some of these difficulties, a delegation of miners asked the Canadian surveyor, William Ogilvie, to work on Bonanza and Eldorado creeks, and he agreed to do so after he had surveyed the Dawson City townsite.

One miner on Eldorado, the former bartender Clarence Berry, with his partner, had bought No. 5 on Eldorado. He learned from Ogilvie that No. 5 was 46½ feet longer than the legal limit. Worse yet, his winter dump of paydirt, estimated to be worth $150,000, was piled up on an adjoining claim which the surveyor declared was now vacant. Berry could not legally stake another claim on this creek, so he

Klondike Hotel, Dawson City, 1898; George Carmack is standing by the doorway, hands folded. (COURTESY SHOREY BOOK STORE, SEATTLE)

persuaded a trusted friend to stake on the fraction, then purchased the fraction from his friend, a perfectly legal transaction.

As a result of the survey, Skookum Jim's No. 1 Above on Bonanza was discovered to be oversize, leaving unoccupied a fractional claim 61 feet in length. Jim's nephew Patsy, now 18 years old, filed on this fractional claim, known as No. 1-A Above. It was recorded in the name of Tagish Patsy on March 1, 1897.

Not until June, after he had been on Bonanza Creek for nine months, did Carmack receive mail from Rose. He promptly sent her and James an invitation to join him on Bonanza. And, at long last, he told his family about Kate and Graphie.

I am well and able to eat my beans three times a day. Well, things are turning out better every day. We drifted out a box and a half length and got $3,000 and we have three more to wash. [A box length of paydirt is all within shoveling distance of a 12-foot sluice box.] I have just put in a big lift wheel to raise the water to sluice with but the water is very low in the creek but this is the dry time of the year.

We sold one of our claims. [Tagish Charley's No. 2 Below.] We got $13,750 and we still have a claim apiece. I could sell out any day for $25,000 for my interest but I can make twice that much and sit around and smoke my pipe. If I had known what I do now, I would have had you and James in here by now.

Bring good rubber overshoes and gum boots, plenty thread and needles and buckskin needles. You can make at least $1,000 here this winter sewing and washing for the miners. My wife had (now don't faint), my wife had more work than she could do all winter but she is getting too high toned to work now.[3]

The rest of his letter gave detailed instructions on what to bring along and how to run the rapids. After signing the letter, Carmack added this postscript.

My wife is Irish and talks very broad English, but I have the prettiest little daughter you ever saw.

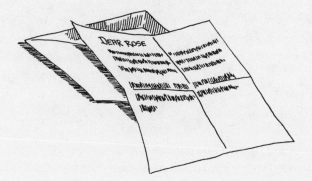

Chapter 9

Payoff in the Klondike

George Carmack's June letter to his sister and her husband did not reach them at their California ranch until August 1897 but newspaper stories about the arrival of the *Excelsior* and the *Portland* had made them aware of the great outpouring of gold from the Klondike. Rose was eager to join her brother on Bonanza Creek but her ailing husband could not travel. Sixty-six-year-old James Watson suffered from a bladder ailment that would prove fatal. The couple declined the trip.

During the winter of 1897–98, Carmack and his two

95

Kate, George and Graphie Carmack in front of their cabin on Bonanza Creek, 1898. (COURTESY KING COUNTY SUPERIOR COURT, SEATTLE)

partners continued their winter mining operations on Bonanza. They hired a dozen men to work underground on all three claims, digging by candlelight. Kerosene was unavailable in Dawson that winter. Candles were scarce and sold for a dollar each, but Carmack's party could well afford them. The richest find by Carmack's men during the daily testing of the paydirt hoisted out of the shaft was a single panful from Skookum Jim's No. 1 Above, which yielded $218 in gold. Any nugget larger than a pea was carefully saved to make watch chains, stickpins, necklaces and other pieces of jewelry for friends and relatives. However, in this remote camp, gold did not always bring comfort and happiness.

One midwinter morning, a Klondike miner named Ed Conrad, out for a Sunday stroll, sauntered along Bonanza Creek. As he approached Discovery Claim, he heard a woman screaming, as though calling for help. Conrad broke into a run. When he came within sight of the Carmack cabin, there stood Kate, gesticulating wildly and yelling in Tagish. Conrad froze, unable to understand her anguished words.

Carmack emerged from the woods, pulling a small sled loaded with firewood.

"What's going on?" asked Conrad.

"Oh that woman," replied Carmack as he began unloading the firewood. "She's just telling me no wood, no fire, no dinner. She thinks her screaming will make me move faster."[1]

When their winter paydirt dumps were sluiced out in the 1898 spring cleanup, Carmack and his Tagish partners received their first big payoff. After their dozen workmen had been paid off and 20% royalty paid to the Canadian government, more than $150,000 in gold remained to be divided among the three men. Then they leased out their three claims to several other miners.

Carmack had not been home in 13 years. He decided to

Birthday party for Mrs. Tozieran, Dawson City, 1898; George Carmack is seated at extreme left. (COURTESY SHOREY BOOK STORE, SEATTLE)

take Kate and Graphie to visit his sister in California, also inviting Skookum Jim, Tagish Charley and Patsy Henderson. With money no longer a problem, the Carmack party chose to travel in comfort, by river steamer to St. Michael and then by ocean steamer to Seattle.

The six travelers left Dawson on the *Portus B. Weare,* arriving at St. Michael in mid-August, where they checked into the Healy Hotel to await the arrival of the next ocean steamer. Most of the gold they carried with them was turned over to the steamship company for safekeeping.

Skookum Jim insisted on keeping in his possession a large canvas poke of gold dust weighing about 36 pounds and worth about $10,000. Carmack advised him to keep it in the hotel safe, but Jim mistrusted strangers and kept the heavy sack in his hotel room.

The Tagish were drinking at every opportunity. Kate had a fondness for liquor, and although Carmack kept close watch on her, she occasionally managed to steal a bottle of whiskey from Jim while he was sleeping it off. Their excessive drinking at St. Michael embarrassed and exasperated Carmack, but he managed to get them aboard the *Roanoke,* with a great feeling of relief.

The ship left St. Michael on August 22, bound for Seattle. Soon after it put to sea, Skookum Jim inspected his heavy poke of gold. It had been tampered with. Someone had emptied the sack, put back in a bottom layer of gold dust, then several pounds of ordinary BB shot, and topped that with another layer of gold dust. Almost half the original contents had disappeared. Carmack estimated Jim's loss at about $4,000 and concluded that the theft had occurred in Jim's hotel room while the Indian was in a drunken stupor.

On the first morning at sea, Carmack was one of only eight passengers who showed up for breakfast, served by ten dining room stewards. The other 192 passengers presumably were seasick. While in St. Michael, Patsy had purchased a vial of liquid seasick remedy, sold to him by a Chinese waiter who peddled Oriental nostrums on the side. Following the instructions of his Chinese friend, Patsy carefully applied a single drop of the medicine to the tip of his tongue and felt so much better that he was able to appear in the dining room for lunch. In the afternoon he persuaded his brother Charley to take a single drop of the magic potion and soon Charley was able to leave his bunk.

Carmack enjoyed the leisurely ocean voyage on the *Roanoke*. Every morning he and Graphie were up early, walking a dozen laps around the main deck before the others had left their beds. Graphie was still wearing the moosehide moccasins made by her mother, but one of her playmates had brand-new button shoes with velvet tops that Graphie fancied. Graphie told her father she wanted shoes like those of her playmate. Carmack promised her he would buy a pair of button shoes when they arrived in Seattle.

"Now! Now!" screamed five-year-old Graphie.

She could not be pacified, so Carmack called on the father of the other girl and bought the shoes for three times their original cost.

As the *Roanoke* approached the wharf in Seattle on August 30, 1898, crowds of curious spectators greeted the ship and its passengers. One friendly onlooker tossed fresh peaches to the passengers crowding the ship's rail, hitting Graphie on the ear, splattering her with peach juice and causing another outburst of screaming.

Carmack and his companions checked in at the Seattle Hotel in the heart of downtown Seattle. Carmack signed the hotel register as Mr. and Mrs. G.W. Carmack and daughter. Ever since they had begun living together, he had treated Kate as his wife, and he continued to do so.

Although only 38, Carmack was not in the best of health. His teeth ached and his gums were swollen. During the ocean voyage, his rheumatism had worsened; even walking had become painful. His first purchase was a cane. Reluctantly, he decided to stay in Seattle until his medical and dental problems cleared up.

While Carmack was consulting a doctor, Kate bought a sealskin coat costing $1,200. Carmack insisted she return it, and Kate threw a tantrum. She became somewhat pacified,

George, Kate and Graphie Carmack during their first visit to California, 1898. (COURTESY ERNEST C. SAFTIG)

however, when Carmack took her to a jewelry store, dumped a handful of big gold nuggets on the counter, and ordered the jeweler to make a nugget necklace for his wife. Carmack also ordered a nugget watch chain for himself. A few days later, Jim, Charley and Patsy were all wearing watch chains made with Klondike gold.

Carmack was looking around at real estate for sale. Consequently, he was unable to keep an eye on his partners at all times. One day when Tagish Charley was alone in his hotel room, quietly nursing a bottle and idly looking out the fifth-floor window, he had a sudden inspiration. He sent a bellboy out to the bank to obtain $500 in half-dollar coins. Then he amused himself by tossing handful after handful out the window. There was a mad scramble in the street below. As the coins bounced around in the street, men dived from the sidewalk to grab for them. Traffic became snarled. The police were called and Charley was ordered to cease and desist or go for a ride in the paddy wagon.

Carmack handled his money more prudently. He deposited $22,000 in the Bank of California and an additional $10,000 in the National Bank of Commerce. In September he purchased a small run-down building, the Togo Hotel, located at 309 Maynard Avenue, paying $2,500 in cash. He bankrolled the G.W. Carmack Company, an auction and commission firm which also handled jewelry, located at 1325 Second Avenue, but his partner was either careless or crooked and the partnership was soon dissolved. Carmack soon discovered that prospecting in the business world was just as unpredictable as panning for gold in the wilderness. His friends and acquaintances from the Klondike were working his poke mighty hard, and he lent money to anyone with a hard-luck story.

Convinced that he still had the golden touch, Carmack looked at several gold-mining properties in the nearby Cascade Mountains. Charley Scheuchzer showed Carmack some hard-rock gold prospects on Granite Mountain, four miles west of Snoqualmie Pass, and Carmack bought six claims from him, 120 acres in area.

By the end of September Carmack's rheumatism had responded to treatment and he threw away his cane. The Carmack party boarded the train for San Francisco, where they checked into the Commercial Hotel. The next day they traveled to his sister's ranch on Tres Pinos Creek, about 80 miles southeast of San Francisco, near Hollister.

There was plenty of room for visitors in the modest ranch-house with the big living room and four bedrooms. Rose was in good health, but James, now white-haired, was barely able to walk. A hired man helped them with the work on the 265-acre spread.

Soon after his arrival, Carmack paid off the mortgage on the ranch. He, Kate and Graphie settled down to spend the winter there.

The Tagish men found ranch life dull. For excitement, Jim shot squirrels, bringing them back to Rose to be made into stew, but she refused to touch them. One day Jim and Charley went to buy a bottle of whiskey in nearby Paicines. They became involved in a drunken fracas with some local ranchers and were still drunk when they returned to the ranch. Rose, a devout Baptist and teetotaler, was horrified. The next day Carmack told his partners they had better start back to the Yukon. They agreed.

Graphie and Kate took an instant liking to ranch life. Graphie delighted in climbing the ancient oak and the two palm trees that shaded the front of the house from the afternoon sun. Mother and daughter ran barefoot through the fields and woods until Carmack explained the danger from rattlesnakes. After seeing her first rattlesnake, which she called "a big worm," Kate took to carrying a revolver. An expert marksman, she loved to shoot the snakes' heads off, bringing the bodies back to the ranch house. Kate called the burros on a neighboring ranch "big jackrabbits." She often went splashing through the creek hunting for red-legged frogs, which she speared.

Proud of her gold-nugget necklace, Kate insisted on wearing it constantly, even on her hunting expeditions. Occasionally she would remove the heavy piece and hang it on the nearest bush or fence post, and then have trouble finding it again.

In March 1899, Kate and George Carmack left the Watson ranch to go north for the spring cleanup on Bonanza. Because they expected to return in a few months, they left Graphie with Rose and James. Again, they stopped in Seattle where Carmack examined some investments. He paid $8,000 cash for a lot with two large houses on the west side of Third Avenue, between Spring and Seneca streets. He also bought an interest in Dr. Peterson's Microbane Hair Grower, guaranteed to cure baldness. This venture failed, but Carmack did very well with his real estate.

The Carmacks sailed from Seattle on the steamer *City of Seattle,* leaving Yesler Wharf on the evening of April 3. At Skagway they boarded the narrow-gauge train of the White Pass & Yukon Railroad, still under construction, rode to the railhead at the summit of White Pass, then traveled by horse-drawn sledge along the winter trail to Dawson.

With the coming of the spring thaw, the 1899 cleanup brought satisfactory results. Once again, Carmack and his partners divided gold worth almost $200,000.

In June, Carmack gave one of his trusted workmen, J. Hutman, a general power of attorney to attend to his interest in No. 1 Below. That summer, he also gave Hutman similar power to look after his Discovery Claim and Skookum Jim's No. 1 Above, although there is nothing in the

Skookum Jim (hand on hip) on his claim, No. 1 Above, 1899. The wood-burning steam boiler and other equipment was used for thawing the frozen soil. (COURTESY NORTHWEST COLLECTIONS, UNIVERSITY OF WASHINGTON, SEATTLE)

mining records to show how Carmack legally came by authority over Jim's claim.

Once again Carmack and his Tagish partners headed for Seattle, but this time they traveled in separate groups. Skookum Jim had built a house for his wife and daughter in the little settlement which had sprung up around the railroad at Caribou Crossing, later called Carcross. Now, he took them Outside with him to help pick out some fancy furniture; Tagish Charley and his wife traveled with them.

The Carmack party included Kate, George and Mary Wilson, Kate's niece. In 1895, Kate's sister had died, leaving Tagish relatives to care for little Mary, her child by miner S.J. Wilson. Kate persuaded Carmack to take the eight-year-old girl to California with them.

Tagish Charley, Skookum Jim and their families arrived

in Seattle aboard the *Topeka* on July 21, 1899. They checked in at their old stomping ground, the Seattle Hotel. Two days later the Carmacks arrived and registered at the Brunswick Hotel.

Carmack went off for a few days to supervise the start of some buildings on his Snoqualmie River mining claim. During his absence, Kate decided to visit her brother Jim at his hotel only a few blocks away. Unfortunately, she had been drinking and the occasion brought her to the attention of the police, the press and the public. According to *The Seattle Post-Intelligencer:*

Mrs. George W. Carmack, the Indian wife of the discoverer of the Klondike, slept last night in the city jail, charged with being drunk and disorderly and disturbing the peace of the city of Seattle. Under the same roof in the men's ward Skookum Jim, her brother, found lodgings as a plain drunk. So much for the debasing tendencies of great wealth and the firewater of the white man.

George W. Carmack, whose wife was arrested while executing an aboriginal Yukon war dance in the second floor corridor of the Seattle Hotel yesterday evening at about 6 o'clock, has a fortune estimated at not less than $200,000 in cash and is, besides, the owner of one of the most valuable claims in the Klondike mining district.

Skookum Jim, his brother-in-law, is also independently wealthy and owns valuable ground in the Klondike. Nevertheless, the possession of mere wealth could not preserve him from being thrown into a dungeon to sleep off his liquor just as though he were an ordinary waterfront Siwash.

Domestic happiness has not been the lot of the Carmack family or its collateral branches since the wealthy squaw man and his relations came down from the north a few months ago to spend the summer in Seattle. Whiskey has had more to do with this unfortunate condition of affairs than anything else, although jealousy is said to have played a part.

It was only three weeks ago that the Carmacks became embroiled over the alleged attentions paid by the husband to women fairer than his dusky spouse. At that time, they were guests at the Hotel Seattle. During the progress of the family jar Mrs. Carmack became so enthusiastic that the police were hastily summoned to prevent what threatened to be a fatal affray. The Carmacks were requested to seek lodgings elsewhere and did so. [There is no truth to this allegation: at that time they were in Dawson.]

Yesterday afternoon Carmack went down Sound in company with a number of business men to look after some investments he has made since leaving the Klondike. Mrs. Carmack, it seems, concluded that the opportunity was ripe for her to make a friendly call on her brother Skookum Jim and Tagish Charley, also a rich man, at their rooms in the Seattle Hotel.

Her visit was ill timed. She found Skookum Jim in tow of a number of gamblers who were priming him with liquor for the purpose, it is said, of getting him in a card game when the right stage of drunkenness was reached. Before the management of the hotel became aware of the fact these men had smuggled in a gallon demijohn and had partially accomplished their object in making Jim drunk.

But it was Jim's wife and the unfortunate Mrs. Carmack who suffered most fully the consequences of their indulgence. Before the supply of liquor was shut off, Mrs. Carmack and her sister-in-law had ceased to discuss Klondike cooking recipes, sub-Arctic management of servants and the utility of polar bear skins in crazy quilts and had strayed into fields far less profitable for argument.

What was the cause of it would be hard to say, but the inevitable quarrel finally came and Mrs. Carmack, remembering the valorous deeds of her forefathers, made a swift grab for her sister's scalp lock. Sister ducked and countered. Then they clinched and hair was madly pulled amid strange northern oaths and imprecations.

Skookum Jim with his wife and daughter, Daisy, ca 1900. (COURTESY YUKON ARCHIVES, WHITEHORSE)

Skookum Jim, who had umpired the fight from the top of a table, declared it a draw but took sides against Mrs. Carmack to the extent of throwing her out of the room and locking the door. From sundry sounds to reach the public from the inside it was judged that the Skookum Jim family then indulged in a little set-to on their own account.

In the meantime the exiled Mrs. Carmack, crooning a wild and warlike melody and punctuating the pauses in the tempo with bits of Indian profanity, started out on a hunt for her absent spouse. In some manner she convinced herself that he had misled her by a false account of his absence from the city, and she began to break in the doors indiscriminately in her search.

The alarmed guests summoned a detachment of bell boys who were able to do nothing with the jealous woman. Fighting with the strength of a wild animal, she was carried down to the entrance of the hotel and there Police Officer Grant, with the assistance of Jailer Corbett, dragged her to the patrol wagon and hauled her off to jail.

At the police station the wife of the Klondike discoverer was searched. Her worldly possessions were found to consist of $120 in gold dust, a gold watch and brass breastpin.

Skookum Jim soon joined his sister at the jail. The last seen of him he was peacefully sleeping on the floor with his arm thrown affectionately about the neck of a drunk picked up in the Mug Saloon.[2]

The following day this brief item appeared in another newspaper:

Mrs. George W. Carmack, the Indian wife of the discoverer of the Klondike, and who is probably the richest

The Hotel Seattle, ca 1905. (COURTESY SEATTLE PUBLIC LIBRARY)

Indian woman in the world, was fined $3.60 by Judge Cann this morning for ·drunkenness. Mrs. Carmack loaded up on champagne last night, and in company with some Indian friends, made Rome howl in the Seattle Hotel. Officer Grant gathered her in, and prosecuted her this morning. She refused to tell who furnished her the champagne.[3]

Mild-mannered Tagish Charley was an accomplished tippler who could drink more than Kate and Jim together without getting himself into trouble. During the Tuesday night roundup the police had ignored him, but not for long. A few days later, Tagish Charley became the subject of another newspaper article.

The troubles of George Carmack's Indian brothers-in-law are never-ending. Yesterday it was Tagish Charley's turn. After the incarceration of his brother, Skookum Jim, and his sister, Mrs. Carmack on Tuesday night for drunkenness, Charley continued his uninterrupted spree in company with several white men of more or less shady reputation.

At about 3 o'clock yesterday afternoon Police Sergeant Ward hauled Charley out of the Seattle Hotel Bar, sharply rebuked him for his riotous conduct and advised him to go home. It seems, however, that Charley continued his potations. Yesterday he appeared at police headquarters and made charges that he had been taken to headquarters on the night previous and robbed. An investigation was made with the result that Tagish Charley's belongings were found in the safe at the Seattle Hotel where he had been induced to leave them at 7 o'clock yesterday morning. They consisted of two gold watches worth $300 each, 27 gold rings, two gold nugget chains each 18 inches long, five huge gold nugget scarf pins, a diamond stud worth fully $300 and $400 in cash. The police say Charley would have been a ripe plum for some highwayman had he strayed away from the hotel before he deposited his valuables with the night clerk.[4]

When Carmack returned to Seattle and learned of the outrageous behavior of his wife and her relatives, he was furious. In his next letter to Rose he described his reaction to their conduct.

Arrived here all safe last Sunday. I have been out looking at the country and just got back. Jim and Charley are here and a nice time they have been making of it.

All hands got drunk and some of them got in the cooler. I am disgusted with the whole outfit. My but the papers had a nice writeup. If they only had the truth and left me out I would not care. I feel like taking an axe and smashing something.

Now don't worry about me. Don't matter what you see in the papers because I don't drink and I don't care what the rest does.

If Kate's trunks were here I would ship her back to Dyea mighty quick. She is getting so unreasonable. I am simply boiling mad now.[5]

Now that Carmack was a wealthy man, he felt entitled to a little peace and comfort after all his years of struggle and hardship. He was also trying to establish himself in the Seattle business community. The unpredictable actions of Kate and her relatives were no help at all. Reluctantly Carmack came to the conclusion that eventually he would have to end his close association with the Tagish, all of them. The process turned out to be long and troublesome.

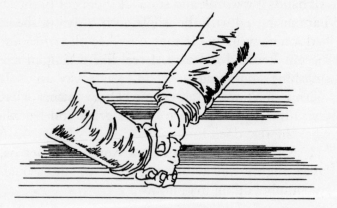

Chapter 10

Marguerite Jumps Kate's Claim

The daughter born in 1874 to Marie and Jacob George Saftig of San Francisco was christened Marguerite Saftig. Her father had accumulated a modest fortune in the real estate business in San Francisco, but when he promoted a gold-mining venture in the Sierra Nevada Mountains, he lost his mine, his money and his wife.

Displaying an early interest in men, mining and moving about, daughter Marguerite married at 14 and became Marguerite Laimee. She traveled in the gold-mining camps of South Africa as Marguerite Laimee, in the gold fields of

Australia as Marguerite Le Grande, in the Klondike as Biddy McCarthy. Eventually, she was to add Carmack to her list of names.

Her marriage to Peter M. Laimee, a zinc molder in a San Francisco foundry, came in 1888. The rocky union lasted less than two years. When Peter began visiting a certain Martha who operated a parlor house on South Market Street, Marguerite left him and went to Spokane, Washington, where she filed suit for divorce. She never went back to find out if the divorce had been made final.

After a stay in the silver-mining camps of the Coeur d'Alene district of Idaho, working as an entertainer, Marguerite and her sister Cecile went to the gold fields of South Africa. From there she went to Melbourne, Australia, accompanied by a man named Joseph Le Grande.

From Sydney, Marguerite sent her mother a picture postcard of the steamer *Oruba,* saying, "This is the steamer that Joe and I came to Sydney, New South Wales, from Melbourne, Australia. Love and million kisses to all at home. Marguerite and Joseph Le Grande."[1]

Years later, Marguerite would deny legal ties to Le Grande. "I knew Joe for many years. He was a man who followed me all over the world; he was very much in love with me, and wanted to marry me, but I never married him," she insisted.[2] Indeed, she set out for the Yukon without him.

The July 21, 1897, edition of *The Sydney Morning Herald* carried an article on gold discoveries in the Yukon as reported by Inspector Charles Constantine of the North-West Mounted Police on November 20, 1896.

On August 19, 1897, the *Australian Mining Record* published excerpts from San Francisco newspapers reporting the arrival of the *Excelsior* and the *Portland* with their gold-laden miners. Klondike miner Clarence Berry was quoted as saying, "Two million dollars taken from the Klondyke region in less than five months, and a hundred times that amount awaiting those who can handle a pick and shovel." The notice got Marguerite's full attention. A veteran stampeder, her good looks still intact, Marguerite decided to go north and get herself a Klondike millionaire. In the spring of 1898 she left Sydney, arriving at Dawson City in July. She brought $2,000 in cash, the proceeds of several years of mining the miners of a dozen camps. Under the name of Marguerite Laimee, she opened a cigar store on the first floor of the Green Tree Saloon and Hotel on Front Street, the main thoroughfare.

On the second floor of the Green Tree Hotel lived several young ladies who provided Klondike miners with services that appeared to be in great demand at all hours of the day and night. As a result of one occupant's carelessness, a fire broke out on the second floor of the hotel, burning it to the

The Green Tree Hotel, Dawson City, 1899. (COURTESY NORTHWEST COLLECTIONS, UNIVERSITY OF WASHINGTON, SEATTLE)

ground. Forty other buildings were destroyed by the fire, gutting the main business district of Dawson City.

After the town was rebuilt, Marguerite reopened her cigar store at Second and Lane, directly opposite the Canadian Bank of Commerce, where many miners fresh from the creeks brought their gold. Mounties who regularly patrolled her establishment called her Biddy McCarthy. Years later, testifying under oath, Marguerite stated that the two cigar stores netted her $60,000 in less than two years. A shrewd businesswoman, she purchased a half-acre lot in the heart of Dawson City for $750 and promptly leased it for $500 a month.

After two years in Dawson City, however, Marguerite had yet to find the Klondike millionaire she hoped for. At 26 years old, she was a charming woman with the bosomy, wasp-waisted figure admired in the era. (One of her cigar-smoking customers said she always looked as if she had just tucked a pair of ostrich eggs in her blouse.)

On June 20, 1900, Marguerite attended a dinner party given by her friends Mr. and Mrs. Joe Collins. Also among the guests was George Carmack, who had traveled north alone that spring, leaving Kate and Graphie with his sister. When Marguerite was introduced to Carmack, she realized that he was the man she had been looking for. Strong-minded and uninhibited by the Victorian conventions of the day, she went after him.

Carmack was fascinated. She was fashionable, her eyes were big and brown, her smile beguiling. Before the evening was over he asked Marguerite to marry him. For several years he had lived with an Indian woman, he explained, but all that was over with now. Eight years of rambling around the world had taught Marguerite to make instant decisions, and she promptly accepted the offer of marriage from 40-year-old Carmack. He said he planned to sell his Klondike mining properties and settle down in Seattle to look after his business interests there. Marguerite said she would dispose of her Dawson City properties and go to Seattle with him.

When Carmack got back to Bonanza Creek, he asked Tagish Charley and Skookum Jim to meet him in Seattle to split up the proceeds of the recent cleanup.

On the first of July, Marguerite and George boarded the riverboat *Yukoner* for the trip upriver past Whitehorse to Caribou Crossing. Here they stayed overnight before taking the White Pass & Yukon train to Skagway. At Skagway they walked up the gangplank of the *City of Topeka* for the voyage along the inland passage to Seattle. Carrying 75 Klondikers and more than a million dollars in Klondike gold, the *City of Topeka* arrived in Seattle on the evening of July 14, 1900. Marguerite went on to Portland to visit her mother, who lived at the Spalding Hotel.

Knowing that when Jim and Charley arrived they would check in at the Seattle Hotel, Carmack made his headquarters at the Hotel Northern. The day after his arrival, he delivered three large canvas pokes of gold to the U.S. Mint assay office, for which he received $20,363.70.

Carmack remained in Seattle for about a week, taking care of his business affairs there before going on to San Francisco. In a letter written shortly after he checked into a San Francisco hotel, Carmack informed Rose of his plans.

> I suppose you think it strange that I do not come straight home. But the fact is, I can't ever live with Kate again; it is simply a misery for me. You may tell Kate so if you like. I will send her some money. Jim and Charley are now in Seattle. If she will go to them, she will get some more when she gets there. I am sorry that this happened but I can't help it. As soon as Kate leaves I

will come home and see you. She must not take Graphie away. If she does, I will take her by law.[3]

When Rose told Kate that Carmack was not coming back to her, she refused to believe it and stubbornly insisted she would stay at the Watson ranch until Carmack returned.

Carmack's letter reached Rose at a time when she was overwhelmed with problems. On several occasions Kate had sneaked away from the ranch and gone on a drunken spree for days at a time, leaving Rose to look after Graphie and Mary Wilson, Kate's niece. The two cousins squabbled constantly. James Watson, now an invalid, required unceasing care. The ranch chores were time-consuming, and Rose wondered whether she should sell the ranch and move to nearby Paicines or Hollister. She decided to ask her brother's advice and telegraphed him to meet her at the Williams Hotel in Gilroy.

When they met, George was reluctant to give his sister a straight yes or no answer about selling the ranch. He promised to consider the matter and advise her later, but only after Kate had gone. He urged Rose to continue trying to get Kate to join Jim and Charley in Seattle.

In mid-August Carmack went back to Seattle to settle up with Skookum Jim and Tagish Charley. Part of their 1900 spring cleanup had been shipped to the assay office in Seattle, where they received higher pay for their gold. Carmack's share was $58,000. Carmack's lawyer had prepared the papers for the transfer of all his holdings in the Klondike to Skookum Jim.

Carmack led his two partners to the office of his Seattle attorney in the Arcade Building. Jim and Charley sat stiffly in their chairs, uncomfortable in their city clothes and the August heat. Carmack's lawyer read aloud the documents transferring Carmack's Discovery Claim and No. 1 Below to Skookum Jim. Terminating their partnership proved to be a complicated affair, requiring the services of lawyers, notaries and stenographers. Their efforts together had spanned many years. Together they had sweated and suffered as they struggled to carry heavy packs across the Chilkoot Pass. Together they had lived in the native village where Jim and Charley had taught Carmack the Indian ways of survival in the Yukon wilderness. Four years ago this very month—was it really that long ago?—standing on the bank of Bonanza Creek, Jim and Charley and George had exchanged handshakes and agreed to divide, share and share alike, all the gold they found. Their trust, the essential element of any partnership, was still strong.

When the attorney finished his reading, he called for signatures. Carmack gave Jim one final bit of advice, reminding him to have the documents promptly recorded when he reached Dawson. Carmack grinned as he shook hands with his partners for the last time. Charley smiled faintly, but Jim's craggy face showed no sign of emotion. Carmack wished them good luck and the three men parted. Skookum Jim and Tagish Charley returned to the Klondike, and Carmack never saw them again.

In his next letter to Rose, Carmack explained the transaction.

> I sold my interest in the Klondike to Jim and I sold it cheap just to get rid of them. I got only $20,000 for my share. I traded it for their share in the Seal Rock Hotel in Seattle. That property brings me in two hundred dollars per month. Now I am going to mortgage it over to you for $30,000, so if Kate wants to get too much, she won't get anything.
>
> This leaves me well and getting fat and happy, only

when I think of you and poor James then I have to swallow that big lump. Well, you know.

From your ever loving brother,

G.W. Carmack

Jim got full the other night and got a free bed in the station house.[4]

When Carmack returned to San Francisco in September, Kate was still at the ranch with Rose, showing no inclination to leave. James Watson's condition continued to worsen. At Carmack's suggestion, Rose rented a house in Hollister so James could receive better medical attention. She took Graphie and Mary with her but told Kate there was no room for her at the Hollister house.

Kate, troubled with an eye infection, was being treated by a physician in Hollister. She told him about being separated from her daughter and the sympathetic physician helped her rent the house next door to Rose.

Chapter 11

Kate Sues for Divorce

Kate had no intimate friends to confide in. Some of her neighbors in Hollister tried to talk to her, but the fractured English and limited vocabulary of the 33-year-old Tagish woman made communication difficult. When gossipers spread the word that Kate's husband was a Klondike millionaire, several neighbors offered to help her. The trusting and unsophisticated native of the Yukon accepted their advice, and on October 2, 1900, her attorney filed a suit for divorce, charging George Carmack with adultery.

Following the advice of his attorney, Carmack continued to avoid meeting Kate. He knew all too well her volatile tongue and unpredictable behavior. A steady, almost daily exchange of letters flowed between Carmack and his sister.

I hope Kate won't try to take the girls away from you. What do they say about her does Graphie ever say anything about me. Would she like to come to me if she had a chance. Do the children need any underwear or anything if they do I will send it to you. Has Graphie got her wheel in town. I want them to look nice and clean never let them go out with soiled clothes. Don't you do their washing, send it to the laundry.[1]

Though Carmack offered advice to Rose, he avoided contact with Graphie directly.

I know it must seem hard on little Pot that I wont write to her but I know she would tell her mother that she got a letter from PaPa then it would get out & then such pumping the child would get & maybee wind up in trouble the less I seem to care for the child the less will be the fight for her.[2]

Carmack wanted to get back to Seattle to look after his business affairs but was obliged to remain close to his San Francisco lawyer. He sent word to Marguerite, still visiting her mother in Portland, to join him. She checked into the Palace Hotel.

In the third week of October Carmack returned to Seattle, accompanied by Marguerite, to make a final inspection of his gold mine in the Cascade Mountains before the autumn snowfall closed the road.

Assured by his attorneys that Kate's lawsuit presented no legal obstacle, Carmack suggested to Marguerite that they be married in a nearby town. She agreed. On October 30, 1900, George Carmack and Marguerite Laimee were wed at St. John's Church in Olympia, Washington. Marguerite's mother, Mrs. Ernest Hardt, and the minister's wife were the only attendants. A few days later the newlyweds were back in San Francisco.

Kate's lawyer in Hollister persuaded her to initiate a second lawsuit, this one directed against Rose Watson, alleging that she had kidnapped Graphie. She asked for $10,000 and return of the child.

Carmack continued to write Rose several times a week. He made certain no one tampered with his letters by sealing each with a dab of black wax and impressing the letter "M" with a ring of Marguerite's. In one letter, he was contemptuous of Kate's kidnapping suit.

> I can't say that I was surprised & I did not know whether to get mad or laugh at such a ridiculas trumped up storey, the whole thing is simply a black mailing scheme, I think they see their bread is all dough with me so they are trying some other plan.[3]

Kate's attorney was unable to locate any documentary evidence of marriage between her and George Carmack. Meanwhile, some of Kate's acquaintances had convinced her that if she dropped the divorce suit, her husband would most likely return to her. Unable to understand the complexities and built-in delays of the white man's legal system, she told her Hollister lawyer she wanted to drop the divorce suit.

In response to the motion, on November 28, 1900, the

judge of the Superior Court of San Benito County ordered that the suit for divorce be dismissed. Graphie and Mary Wilson were returned to Kate and the kidnapping charges against Rose were dropped.

Carmack did not appear distressed in a November letter to Rose.

> I hate to see her take the child but I dont think she will keep her very long. As soon as I can get her to sign an agreement to release me then I can look after the child.[4]

Kate never signed an agreement releasing Carmack from any claims she might have against him, and Graphie did not return to his care until she was in her teens.

James Watson's lingering illness finally came to an end December 7, 1900. Carmack did not attend his funeral, but Marguerite did, accompanied by her younger brother Jacob. It was the first meeting of Jacob Saftig, 22, and Graphie Carmack, seven. Ten years later they would marry.

Carmack continued to write frequently to Rose, offering to "put up a nice headstone" over James' grave.[5] Ever the businessman, in a letter written a week after James' death he asked Rose to locate and send him his Microbane Medical Company stock certificates.

> I will send you some of their printed matter, and if you see any of your friends whose hair is falling out, or if they have dandruff the Microbane will cure it without fail, and it will grow hair on bald heads if directions are carefully followed You need not be afraid to recomend it.[6]

On January 13, 1901, Kate's San Francisco attorney, John H. Durst, filed a suit for separate maintenance in the courts of San Francisco.

Carmack wrote to Rose about the new lawsuit.

> Well I gues the enemy only let go just to spit on their hands so they could get a better hold I see by the papers that there is another suit against me for maintenance so I guess the thing will come in court this time and be settled for good.[7]

A month later George Carmack made a lengthy deposition, over 70 pages, relating under oath the details of his 13-year association with Kate. Attorney Durst made a fruitless search for some evidence of a marriage ceremony between Kate and Carmack.

As the months rolled by without a trial of the separate maintenance suit, Kate grew increasingly impatient. In July of 1901, she abandoned the lawsuit and left Hollister, taking the two girls with her. In Seattle, they were joined by Tagish Charley, who escorted them back to the Yukon.

Chapter 12

The Tagish Village at Caribou Crossing

When Skookum Jim, Charley and Kate returned to the Yukon, the Tagish village where they had grown up had moved. In 1898 the White Pass & Yukon Route had begun building a railroad connecting the salt-water port of Skagway with the town of Whitehorse on the Yukon River. The 110-mile narrow-gauge track through White Pass was completed in 1900.

A railroad bridge spanned the shallow stream between Lake Bennett and Nares Lake at the spot where the caribou crossed, and the construction camp built at this location grew into a settlement appropriately named Caribou Crossing. Some of the Tagish Indians worked on the railroad during construction, while others hunted caribou to feed the workers. The Indians soon became accustomed to the white man's food and clothing, which they bought at the Caribou Crossing trading post. By the time the railroad was completed, most of the Indians at the Tagish village had abandoned their homes there, moving to a new site on the shore of Nares Lake, just across the railroad bridge from the white man's settlement. Skookum Jim and Tagish Charley were among them.

The house that Jim had built for his wife and daughter, Daisy, was the finest in the village. Constructed with mill-sawed lumber, it included a large living room, dining room and a wide porch as well as the usual kitchen and several bedrooms. It was heated by a wood stove and lighted by kerosene lamps. Water was carried in a bucket from Nares Lake, only a few yards away.

Jim furnished his house ornately. The chairs for his dining-room table had mother-of-pearl inserts. His silverware was encrusted with gold nuggets taken from his Bonanza mine. On a trip to Vancouver, Jim had spent $2,000 on a Persian rug with an ornate floral design. When the rug arrived and was laid out on the living-room floor, it was two feet wider than the room. Jim was ready to cut the rug, but his wife would not permit it, so he found a better solution: building an extension on the house. Sixty years later the house still stood, the joints in the roof and siding where the extension had been added clearly visible.

In the summer of 1901, Kate, Graphie and Mary Wilson returned to the Yukon, escorted by Tagish Charley. Later Skookum Jim built a cabin for his sister and gave her money to live on.

Eight-year-old Graphie attended the mission school that

Skookum Jim (holding gold pan) with his wife and daughter, Daisy, in front of their house at Carcross, 1901; the man in the white shirt is Tagish Charley. (COURTESY NORTHWEST COLLECTIONS, UNIVERSITY OF WASHINGTON, SEATTLE)

Bishop William C. Bompas of the Anglican church had established for Tagish children at Caribou Crossing. An accomplished linguist and scholar, Bishop Bompas had already translated the New Testament into four Indian languages. He read biblical studies written in ancient Syriac and Greek, translating them into English.

When his educational and clerical duties permitted, the bishop enjoyed meeting the trains that stopped at Caribou Crossing. Passengers gawked at the tall, bearded, ascetic-looking man in the long black frock coat, carrying a small leather bag on a shoulder strap, who strode up and down the station platform in this tiny outpost of civilization.

His extensive correspondence with church officials and others brought Bishop Bompas considerable mail, which was frequently misdirected to the Cariboo mining district of British Columbia. Irked by this mis-routing, the bishop wrote a letter to the Canadian Board on Geographical Names at Ottawa, calling attention to the confusion resulting from the similarity of the names Cariboo and Caribou Crossing. He requested that the name Caribou Crossing be changed to Carcross, and government officials made the change.

Graphie Carmack inherited her father's love of roaming. One sunny summer day, Graphie, Jim's daughter Daisy and another Tagish girl named Sha-kuni sneaked aboard the White Pass & Yukon train at Carcross and rode the 43 miles to Whitehorse without being approached by the conductor. A Mountie found the children wandering around town and took them to police headquarters, where they spent the night. In the morning, they returned to Carcross on the train.

In 1905, Skookum Jim paid the annual tuition fee of $300 for Graphie to attend the mission school at Whitehorse, where she lived with the Reverend Isaac O. Stringer and his family. One day Graphie persuaded the Stringer girl, also 12, to accompany her on a visit to the red-light district of Whitehorse. The girls of the line were pleased to have such unusual visitors, even more so when they learned that one girl was the daughter of a clergyman. The girls returned home wearing wide, frilly hats and loaded down with gifts of candy, cookies and an assortment of hair ribbons. When Mrs. Stringer learned the source of all these luxuries, she grabbed all the gifts and threw them on the fire.

Following Jim's example, Tagish Charley also built a new home at Carcross. In the summer of 1901, while in Seattle to meet Kate, he ordered a heavy Brussels carpet, an upholstered sofa and chair, a solid mahogany dining-room set and costly furnishings. His was the second most elaborately furnished house in the village.

To distinguish him from several other Charleys living at Carcross (including one other Tagish Charley), the man who had been Carmack's companion became known as Dawson Charley. Adding to the confusion, Dawson Charley and the other Tagish Charley were married to sisters.

Dawson Charley bought the Carcross Hotel across the channel from the native village and hired someone to run it for him. Then he settled down to do a little drinking and some serious gambling. A compulsive gambler, he gradually dribbled away his fortune. Any cash that reached him had a life expectancy no greater than that of the smoke rings he blew from his pipe. Professional gamblers repeatedly got Charley drunk and then fleeced him with their crooked dice and card games. When Charley ran out of cash, he would toss one of his numerous nugget stickpins or diamond rings on the gaming tables.

As was the custom, Dawson Charley celebrated the Christmas holiday in 1908 by having a few drinks with friends and relatives. He may have taken a few beyond his limit, for early on the morning of December 26, while crossing the railroad bridge at Carcross, he fell into the open water and was drowned. His body, which had drifted under the ice, was not recovered for several days. He was 42 years old. A large sign at the entrance to the Carcross cemetery states that Dawson Charley was one of the original discoverers of gold in the Klondike.

Skookum Jim fared better. During the fall and winter months, he lived at Carcross, where he wore caribou-skin clothing while hunting with his neighbors or participating in the Tagish ceremonial dances. When he returned to the Klondike each year for the spring cleanup, he walked the streets of Dawson wearing a tailor-made suit and a white shirt, a heavy nugget watch-chain draped across his vest and a large nugget stickpin in his tie. He ate steak in Dawson's best restaurant, washing down his meal with copious drafts of beer or whiskey.

Skookum Jim and Dawson Charley each had sold a half-interest in their claims to a mining partner, G. D. Bentley. With Bentley looking after day-to-day mining operations, Jim was free to spend many of his days and nights in the saloons of Dawson. All too often the Mounties jailed him for being drunk and disorderly. Jail inmates were usually put to work chopping firewood for the police barracks. Jim spent many days in the Dawson jail, where he acquired the dubious distinction of being the best-dressed man working on the "King's woodpile."

On one occasion a Mountie asked Jim how many times he had been arrested.

"One thousand times," Jim answered.

"One thousand times?" echoed the disbelieving Mountie.

"Yes. What's the matter? You jealous?" Jim said.[1]

The richest man in the village of Carcross, Skookum Jim was beseiged by relatives and friends looking for loans and handouts. Because he listened to all and gave to most, his fortune was rapidly dwindling.

Church officials in Whitehorse, aware of Jim's frailties as well as his concern for the welfare of his wife and daughter, persuaded him to sign a series of wills, and later to establish a trust fund. The first will, dated January 11, 1904, bequeathed $5,000 to his wife and appointed a guardian for nine-year-old Daisy. The balance of the estate was bequeathed to Daisy when she reached the age of 21. Jim also requested that his executors look after the education of his daughter so she could take her place in the white man's society.

By 1904, many of the placer claims in the Klondike were nearing depletion. Big mining companies were buying up claims and reworking the ground with more sophisticated hydraulic and dredging systems. On May 20, 1904, Skookum Jim sold his Klondike mines to the Lewis River Mining and Dredging Company for $65,000. He never went back to the Klondike. His wife left him in 1905 and returned to her Chilkoot people near Dyea.

Jim set up the trust fund church officials had sought, depositing $20,000 to provide for his daughter and help other Indians after her death. Daisy remained at school in Whitehorse and Jim continued to support her with income from the fund.

During the next ten years, Jim spent nearly every summer out in the hills, unsuccessfully searching for gold along the Teslin, Pelly, McMillan, Stewart and Liard rivers.

In the winter of 1915–16, Jim suffered from a bladder ailment. After being hospitalized in Juneau and Whitehorse, he realized his health was failing rapidly and went home to Carcross to die.

On April 4, 1916, Skookum Jim signed another will, the final one, using his legal name of James Mason. His trustees were instructed to pay $1,000 to his sister Kate Carmack, $1,000 to Patsy Henderson; $1,000 to a cousin, Caribou John, and $500 to a Tagish Jim. The trust fund that had paid for Daisy's education was to be known as the Skookum Jim Indian Fund.

The fund trustees were instructed that "... the income from said trust fund shall be devoted towards furnishing medical attendance, supplying necessities and comforts to Indians in the Yukon Territory and towards assisting needy and deserving Indians in said Territory in any way or manner said Trustees may deem best." The bishop of the Anglican church in the Yukon and the commissioner of the Yukon Territory and their respective successors were made trustees of the will and trust fund.

After the will was taken care of, Jim sent for his daughter, who was studying drama in San Francisco. Daisy had been fed beer at the age of two and was now a 25-year-old alcoholic. When Daisy arrived in Carcross to attend her father during his terminal illness, Jim told her his final requests. He wanted to be buried in a brand-new white man's suit and in a white man's casket shipped from Vancouver, not in a box built by his Tagish relatives.

Skookum Jim died July 11, 1916, aged 60. With his assets tied up in the trust fund, his Carcross home was sold for $275 to pay burial expenses. Daisy saw to his burial in a new suit and a casket purchased from the Taylor and Drury store in Whitehorse. A stone monument marking his grave in the hilltop cemetery at Carcross bears the name that George Carmack gave him: James Mason.

Kate Carmack at Carcross, 1919.

Kate Carmack's cabin at Carcross. (COURTESY SHOREY BOOK STORE, SEATTLE)

Largely dependent on Skookum Jim for support, Kate Carmack led a lonely and embittered life after she returned to Carcross. She lived in a small cluttered cabin on the shore of Nares Lake, where she chopped her own wood and carried her water from the lake. For a time she sewed moccasins and fur mittens, selling them to summer tourists at the train depot. When drinking, which was often, she liked to tell visitors how she, not George Carmack, discovered gold on Bonanza. Occasionally an eager writer picked up her story, embellished it with a few more details, and proclaimed to the world that Kate was the true discoverer, not knowing she was encamped 15 miles away at the mouth of the Klondike at the time.

A beautiful girl just out of her teens when she met Carmack, she retained her good looks well into her 30s but uncontrolled drinking caused that beauty to fade. By the time she was 40 she had gained weight, become slovenly in appearance, and aged rapidly.

When the influenza epidemic of 1920 swept the Yukon, Kate became one of the victims. Her influenza turned into pneumonia and after a ten-day illness, she died on March 29. Graphie left her Berkeley home and returned to Carcross to pick up her mother's few belongings, which included some family photographs and the nugget necklace that George Carmack had given her many years before.

Kate was buried in an unmarked grave in the Carcross cemetery. In 1958 it was covered with brush. Scrawled on a piece of plywood were these words:

Kate Carmacks
63 years old
Died March 29, 1920

Kate often referred to herself as Mrs. Carmacks rather than Mrs. Carmack. Her age was probably estimated by relatives, for no record of the date of her birth exists. In 1901, in a sworn deposition, George Carmack stated that Kate was about 20 when he first met her in 1887. That would have made her 26 years old when her daughter was born and 53, not 63, when she died. In 1968 the crude board marker on her grave was replaced with a fine stone monument, paid for by public subscription.

Daisy Mason died in 1938, but her father's trust fund, wisely managed by church trustees, continued to grow. In 1965, in accordance with Skookum Jim's instructions that the money be used for the benefit of the Indians of the Yukon valley, a portion of the money was used to begin construction of the Skookum Jim Friendship Centre in Whitehorse. Today, it is a place of great informality where Yukon Indians can drop in at any time and in any condition. The sign on the door tells it all: "Welcome to Skookie's."

Patsy Henderson, who was with Kate and Graphie at the mouth of the Klondike at the time of the discovery on Bonanza, outlived all his relatives. For many years the White Pass & Yukon Route employed him to meet their trains at Carcross during the summer tourist season. Dressed in caribou-skin clothing made by his wife Edith, Patsy would tell listeners the story of the discovery of gold on "Bonanzy" and sing Tagish songs while beating his Indian-style drum. He outlived his brother, Tagish Charley, by more than half a century. In 1966, Patsy suffered a stroke and was taken to the Whitehorse Hospital where he died on February 11. He was 87.

Edith and Patsy Henderson at Carcross, 1959. (PHOTOGRAPH BY THE AUTHOR)

Chapter 13

The Peaceful Seattle Years

In the spring of 1901, Marguerite and George Carmack left
California for Seattle and moved into the Fremont Hotel, a
four-story brick building Carmack owned.

Apprehensive that Kate's attorneys might attempt to at-
tach his Seattle real estate, Carmack deeded all his property
to Marguerite, who promptly changed the name of the Fremont Hotel to the Carmack Annex. While Carmack was
busy looking after his gold mine in the Cascades, she operated the Carmack Annex as a lodging house. A capable and
innovative manager, she supervised a year-long renovation

of the building.

With the purchase of a Mobile Steamer, Carmack became a pioneer Seattle automobile owner. Made by the Mobile Company of America at Tarrytown, New York, his four-seater open Runabout Model was powered by a 14-inch steam boiler and steered with a tiller.

Carmack was one of the first to make the trip from Seattle to San Francisco by automobile. Accompanied by Marguerite, he left Seattle in September 1902 in the kerosene-burning Steamer. Driving over roads intended for horse and buggy, stopping every 50 miles to fill the water tank, they made slow progress. Occasionally Carmack had to clear away overhanging branches before the automobile could get through, but they completed the journey in 22 days.

George and Marguerite Carmack in their Mobile Steamer. (COURTESY NORTHWEST COLLECTIONS, UNIVERSITY OF WASHINGTON, SEATTLE)

Carmack still had gold fever. In 1899 he had organized the Carmack Gold & Copper Mining Company to develop his hard-rock gold mine about 40 miles east of Seattle in the Cascade Mountains. For the next decade, his major goal was to get that lode mine into production.

Though Carmack had 15 years of practical placer mining behind him, the Cascade mine was a different sort of venture. The hard-rock mining enterprise would require the expenditure of large sums of money before any gold could be recovered.

The main vein of gold-bearing ore was about nine feet wide and three feet thick, assaying about $40 per ton. By the summer of 1900, Carmack's men had constructed a cookhouse, bunkhouse, blacksmith shop and barn at the site. The only access to the mine was by a county road from North Bend, 22 miles away. It was in poor condition, making it almost impossible to haul heavy loads. Carmack wrote a letter complaining to the King County Commissioners, and soon afterward, county crews went to work improving the road. At the time, three shifts of miners kept tunneling operations going 24 hours a day.

While small samples of ore had been sent out for assays, the first shipment of ore was not made until the summer of 1901. Twenty tons taken from three mineralized veins were shipped to the smelter, yielding $1,200 in gold and silver. Carmack was disappointed but not despondent over the relatively small return. He knew he did not have the richest mine in the world, but firmly believed that it could be developed into a profitable operation.

Marguerite took a more pessimistic view. "You couldn't make any money on that mine if you fell into the shaft at ten dollars a foot," she told him on one occasion.[1]

After Carmack had spent about $30,000 on the venture, Marguerite was unable to resist the temptation to give him a

George Carmack at his gold mine on the Snoqualmie River, Washington, ca 1902. (COURTESY ROBERT N. DE ARMOND)

little advice. Since her own father had been a mining promoter, she knew how speculative mining ventures were usually financed.

"Lovie, stop spending your money on the mine or we'll go broke," she told her husband. "Sell stock to the public and use that money to develop the mine."[2]

Carmack took her advice. The Carmack Gold & Copper Mining Company opened an office in the Arcade Building in Seattle and sold stock at 25¢ a share. The sale did not bring in enough money to sustain a large-scale operation, however, and in 1903 Carmack closed the mine. A disgruntled former employee started a fire and the mine buildings burned to the ground. Still, Carmack wasn't daunted. The next year buildings were put up and tunneling work was resumed.

Carmack enjoyed life at the mine. In 1907, he wrote to Rose about it.

> It is nice in the mountains in the summer. I dont like the city we never come out of the hills only on business or grub. I have just finished building a bridge across the river at my camp. The main span was fifty feet, it is built from one big rock to another and nearly 20 ft above the water it is right over some falls and it looks quite romantic.[3]

Although Carmack continued to work the mine each summer for a number of years, and hung onto his gold claims in the Cascades as long as he lived, the mine never got into production again. The first shipment of ore was also the last.

After the Carmack Annex had been remodeled and leased out, the Carmacks moved into the Togo Hotel on Maynard Avenue. Marguerite renovated the building and renamed it Carmack House, and her brother, Jacob Saftig, came up from San Francisco to manage the property. With the exception of the mine in the Cascades, all of Carmack's properties in the Seattle area were firmly under Marguerite's control.

She negotiated the sale of the Seal Rock Hotel for $65,000 cash. That was more than twice what Carmack had paid for it and the money was put to work almost immediately. The Carmacks later purchased a more spacious home, closer to the downtown business district, at 1522 East Jefferson Street, a three-story frame house with 12 rooms and a separate garage at the back of the lot.

Late in 1909, Carmack and his wife decided to build a large apartment building at 170 Eleventh Avenue, only a few blocks from their new home, to be known as the Carmack Apartments. The plans called for a four-story building divided into 29 apartments, 110 rooms in all. Marguerite bossed the construction job while Carmack busied himself with his mine.

Carmack took a course in surveying and learned how to use a surveyor's transit and to draw maps. He told a newspaper reporter, "I am convinced that there are enormous gold deposits in the Cascades and gold will be found when somebody with nerve enough to dig deep goes after it."[4]

That never happened, but Carmack did find his longed-for niche in the Seattle business community. Early in 1909 he commissioned a unique telegraph key to be fabricated according to his instructions. A Seattle jeweler fastened 22 nuggets to a standard telegraph key mounted on a base of Alaskan marble.

When the A-Y-P Exposition opened in Seattle on June 1, thousands of visitors were on hand for the commencement ceremonies. In the East Room of the White House, President Taft tapped Carmack's nugget-studded key, sending a few fluttering clicks across the continent to a telegraph instrument on the speaker's platform in Seattle. Then a cannon boomed as a hundred-foot American flag was unfurled in back of the stage.

More than 3,000,000 people visited the A-Y-P Exposition during its five-month existence. Throughout this period, the Carmack residence, then at 3001 Denny Way, was filled with house guests. Marguerite's mother, Marie Hardt, came up from Portland. Jacob Saftig, Marguerite's younger brother, came from San Francisco. Carmack invited his daughter, then a 16-year-old schoolgirl at Whitehorse, to visit him and see the exposition. Graphie

George Carmack, 1909, wearing a souvenir Alaska-Yukon-Pacific Exposition pin. (COURTESY ERNEST C. SAFTIG)

came, intending to stay only a month, but more than a decade went by before she saw the Yukon again.

During the eight years that Graphie had attended the mission schools at Carcross and Whitehorse, she saw her mother infrequently, a situation that caused her no unhappiness. Long before she became a rebellious teenager, Graphie had rejected her Tagish mother. Eager to escape from the Yukon and her Indian relatives and heritage, she gladly accepted her father's invitation to come to Seattle and see the exposition.

She was developing into a real beauty. She had inherited her mother's doe-like eyes and also a touch of her fiery disposition, although her temper was not quite so volatile. Unlike her mother, Graphie easily adapted to life in the non-Indian world, and she soon fell in love with a white man. Marguerite's brother, Jacob George Saftig, was the tallest man Graphie had ever met, six feet five inches in height, with handsome blue eyes and wavy brown hair. Living in the same house, she saw a great deal of him, and Marguerite encouraged the romance.

At a ceremony in her father's home, on June 30, 1910, Graphie Grace Carmack, 17, married Jacob George Saftig, 32. The newlyweds moved into the Carmack Apartments, where they remained for several years. When their first

Family gathering at the Carmack home in Seattle, ca 1910. Front row: George Carmack in center. Second row: Marguerite's mother, Marie Saftig Hardt at left; Marguerite second from left. Back row: Jacob Saftig at left; Graphie Carmack second from left. (COURTESY NORTHWEST COLLECTIONS, UNIVERSITY OF WASHINGTON, SEATTLE)

child was born, they named him Ernest Charles Saftig. Graphie also gave her son the Tagish name of Kaish, meaning Lone Wolf.

In the fall of 1911, Marguerite and Jacob traveled to Dawson and Carcross. Carmack remained in Seattle, still avoiding Kate, but Marguerite and Jacob called on her in her small, cluttered cabin. Kate ignored Marguerite and refused to take the money Jacob offered her, saying it was Carmack money. Marguerite gave her some clothes and a big hat, which Kate later wore.

In a rambling letter written in 1912, Carmack told Rose about his health and interests.

> There has just been completed an 18 story building and the foundation laid for a 42 story building so you see Seattle is growing a little. I have just had the Automobile overhauled and painted so it is just the same as new, We were in hopes that we would get a chance to make a little trip through California this spring with it, but the way things turned out we could not get away, but we hope for better luck next year. every body is in good health I weigh nearly two hundred pounds so you see I am not worrying very much as to my health and Margie always beats me just a little as to avoirdupois. but when I get to swinging an ax or hammering a drill for a few weeks it will take off some of that surplus weight then I will feel better.[5]

Five years after James Watson died, Rose married Frank Curtis, the hired hand on her ranch, and in 1913 Marguerite and George Carmack went to California to visit the couple. While there, Carmack traveled to the Mother Lode country on the western slope of the Sierra Nevada Mountains. A few mines in the area were still being worked on a small scale, and near the little mining settlement of Westville, high in the mountains, Carmack found some mining properties which he believed were worth developing. Marguerite urged him to buy them. Instead, he leased the property.

Back in Seattle again, Carmack became concerned about what would happen to his estate when he died. Quite fond of Graphie and her two children, Ernest, three and Marguerite, two, he wanted his daughter to have half of his property.

He was worried about possible claims on his estate by Kate, since no court had ever ruled on whether or not his relationship with her constituted a legal marriage, and he consulted his attorney. Carmack wanted to make absolutely certain that his estate would be divided between Graphie and Marguerite, with Kate excluded. His attorney prepared a will, which he assured Carmack was a foolproof way to accomplish his objective. On February 17, 1914, Carmack signed a remarkable document consisting of only two sentences.

> In the name of God, Amen. I, George Washington Carmack, being of sound mind and memory, do make and publish this my last will and testament, that is to say: I devise my property according with the statutes of descent of the State of Washington.[6]

Carmack spent the summer of 1914 working at his gold mine in the Cascades. Marguerite stayed in Seattle to look after their hotel and apartment house properties, which were now bringing in an income of almost $1,000 a month. They kept in touch by letter.

By 1917, Carmack had just about given up hope of ever getting his Cascade mine onto a paying basis. He decided to close it, move to California, and do some prospecting in the Westville area.

Chapter 14

Carmack Continues
His Search for Gold

After three summers of poking around with pick and shovel
on his leased claims in California, Carmack decided to buy
the properties. He had panned enough coarse gold to justify
further development. On August 17, 1917, the 21st anniversary of the day he had staked Discovery Claim on Bonanza Creek, Carmack purchased a group of mining claims
from Leo and Aline Harris.

The three placer claims were in Placer County, not far
from Westville. The largest one, the Snowshoe Mining
Claim, covered 160 acres. The Pacific Blue Lead Mining

Claim was 130 acres and the Outbreak Mining Claim was 40 acres.

In the fall of 1917, Marguerite made another of her periodic trips to Seattle to look after their real estate there. Carmack remained in California, busy with his new mining ventures. In a November letter to her husband, Marguerite expressed her concern about his health.

> Dear Lovie, That pussing you have comes from rotten roots of your teeth. It's very dangerous. Now you attend to it, as you are getting very thin. You have no idea how much I worry about you. I remain your loving wife. 50,000 kisses.
>
> Marguerite[1]

By the next summer, Carmack had a sizable mining operation under way on his Pacific Blue Lead claim. Ten workmen were putting up buildings and digging in search of the elusive paystreak. Graphie's husband, Jacob Saftig, who was between jobs, came up to work too, bringing his family with him. By this time, the Saftigs had three children, Ernest, seven, Marguerite, six, and James George, three.

Marguerite proved to be a remarkable woman. She did all the cooking (at Carmack's insistence, the workmen ate first, then the Carmack family). She also helped with work in the mine, usually wearing men's breeches and knee-high leather boots. One evening while she was preparing supper, padding around the kitchen in her stocking feet, she heard a loud grunting noise outside. Opening the door, she saw a large black bear nosing around the garbage dump. Grabbing a chunk of stovewood, she ran out to the dump in her stocking feet and walloped the bear on the nose. The bear ran off into the woods.

Little Ernest Saftig liked to hang around the blacksmith

shop. One day the blacksmith placed a red-hot prospector's pick on the anvil to cool, and Ernest tried to pick it up. Screaming with pain, he ran to Marguerite. After dipping the boy's hand in a barrel of flour, Marguerite grabbed her husband's rifle and ran out to the blacksmith shop.

"You're fired! Get going!" she told the startled man.

As the blacksmith started down the road to town, Marguerite fired a few shots in his direction until he broke into a run.

About once a week during the summer, the gold-laden paydirt was run through a sluice box. During the cleanup, Carmack chased everyone away while he and Saftig scooped up the accumulated gold. Although the yield was substantial, it was not as great as the cleanups Carmack had obtained on Bonanza Creek.

In the spring of 1919, Marguerite made another business trip to Seattle. On her return to California, she chose to travel by ocean steamer. Shortly before the *Admiral Schley* sailed from Seattle on May 27, Marguerite came aboard with a case of champagne as part of her room baggage. Her roommate, Mrs. Victor Ducette, soon discovered that Marguerite liked to smoke cigars in the privacy of her stateroom.

Early in 1920, Rose and Frank Curtis sold their Tres Pinos Ranch and bought a house in Hollister. Carmack helped them move.

Although Carmack liked to dress up for social gatherings, most of the time he wore work clothes, puffing on a cigar while his neighbors were smoking cigarettes rolled from sacks of Bull Durham tobacco.

Carmack spent the Fourth of July, 1921, with Graphie and Jacob Saftig at their home in Oakland. Saftig was then working as a traveling salesman. Graphie prepared a dinner with some of her father's favorite dishes: pork chops and spinach, with strawberry shortcake for dessert. Carmack always broke out in a rash after eating strawberries but he enjoyed them so much he ate them anyway.

For several years Marguerite had been trying to persuade her husband to write a book about his experiences in Alaska and the Yukon. Carmack made a start on the book project by writing up his Bonanza Creek discovery and the events that immediately preceded it. His narrative ran about 20 typewritten pages. He worked the material over several times, using parts of it while speaking to groups such as the Masons and other fraternal organizations.

Carmack accompanied Marguerite on her May 1922 trip to Seattle. He was a member of the Seattle Lodge of the Yukon Order of Pioneers; Marguerite belonged to a group called the Ladies of the Golden North. They attended a meeting of the Seattle organization and then went to Vancouver, B.C., where Carmack had been invited to speak on May 30 to the Vancouver Cabin of the Yukon Order of Pioneers.

About 30 old-time prospectors from the Klondike were in the audience when Carmack addressed the meeting in O'Brien Hall. Instead of giving an informal talk, as he had done so many times in the past, he read the one and only chapter he had written for his book. It was, Carmack said, the true story of his Bonanza Creek discovery, read in public for the first time.

At the conclusion of his speech, the organization passed a resolution declaring Carmack to be the man who started the Klondike Gold Rush with his August 17, 1896, staking of Discovery Claim on Bonanza Creek. After the meeting, over a supper of bacon and beans, Carmack had a chance to chat with old friends from the Yukon. Some he had known during his trading-post days at Five Finger Rapids. Others had been his neighbors in the Klondike, at Fortymile or elsewhere along the Yukon. For a brief hour or two, Carmack and his pioneer friends recalled and relived the exciting days of their golden past.

When Carmack awoke the next morning, a Wednesday, he realized he was coming down with a chest cold. In addition to frequent spells of coughing, he felt slightly giddy. He remained in his room at the Hotel Vancouver throughout the day, and at Marguerite's insistence, he drank great quantities of hot lemonade.

On Thursday morning, Carmack's cold was worse and he was complaining of chills, saying he felt as if there were a weight on his chest. Marguerite called a doctor. After examining him, Dr. S. Petersky gave Carmack a prescription for cough medicine and advised him to stay in bed until he felt better.

By Friday morning, Carmack's condition had worsened. His face was flushed with fever, his coughing became more painful, and he had to fight for every breath, just as he had done the first time he struggled over the crest of the Chilkoot Pass so long ago. Dr. Petersky examined him again and diagnosed Carmack's illness as lobar pneumonia. He recommended that Carmack be moved to a hospital where he could receive constant medical attention. Marguerite made the arrangements. Just before the ambulance arrived, Carmack took off the diamond-studded gold ring Marguerite had given him on their wedding day and handed it to her.

"Take care of this 'til I get back," he said.[2]

Carmack was taken to Roycroft Hospital at 1036 Haro Street. Marguerite hired special nurses to look after her husband day and night.

Despite the efforts of Dr. Petersky and the other physicians attending him, Carmack's condition grew worse over the weekend. Marguerite stayed in the hospital room with him most of the time, only returning to her hotel for a few hours of sleep during the early morning hours.

By Monday morning, Carmack's heavy breathing became more labored and painful, and he was too weak to talk. During that afternoon, June 5, 1922, the 61-year-old Carmack lay quietly on his hospital bed, motionless except for the opening and closing of his eyes. The once bright blue eyes were now quite dull. At a quarter to six, George Washington Carmack closed his eyes for the last time and his agonized breathing stopped. His life-long quest for gold was ended.

Epilogue

For more than half a century, George Carmack's body was to lie in an unmarked grave.

Alone in Vancouver after Carmack's death, with no relatives or intimate friends to assist her, an exhausted Marguerite had no time to mourn. She sent a brief telegram to Rose and then made arrangements to have her husband's body transported to Seattle.

Several hundred friends and acquaintances attended the funeral for George Carmack, which was held at the Masonic Temple in downtown Seattle on July 9, 1922. Neither Graphie nor Rose was there. Graphie, then living in Oakland, learned of the death of her father from a newspaper article. Seeking more information, she telephoned Rose. Rose, who had not yet seen the newspaper accounts, had little information to offer. She read to Graphie the two-word telegram she had received from Marguerite: "George dead."[1]

Soon after Carmack died, Marguerite was appointed administratrix of his estate. She swore that she was a resident of the state of Washington and that she was the sole legal heir to his estate.

A few weeks later, Rose Curtis and Graphie Saftig petitioned the Superior Court of King County to have the widow removed as administratrix, claiming that Marguerite was not a resident of the state of Washington and that Graphie was one of the legal heirs to the estate. Marguerite immediately resigned her post and the court appointed

Herman S. Frye as administrator. Strapped for money while the estate was tied up in probate proceedings, Marguerite could not even afford to purchase a tombstone for her husband's grave.

When Marguerite filed her final report with the court, she stated that the estate consisted solely of some stock in the Carmack Gold & Copper Mining Company, having an estimated value of $1,000. The new administrator filed exceptions to Marguerite's report, asserting that a large amount of valuable real estate belonging to the estate had come into the hands of Mrs. Carmack and had not been inventoried or accounted for.

Judge King Dykeman presided over the five-day hearing in which 308 pages of testimony were taken. He issued a citation requiring Marguerite to appear and answer questions about the estate. Marguerite expertly parried the questions put to her concerning her murky past. Her evasiveness continually irritated Judge Dykeman. He had taken part in the Klondike stampede, and he knew what went on in the back rooms of saloons and cigar stores.

Marguerite testified that after she met Carmack in 1900, at no time did he ever have more than $30,000 in his possession, and that he soon lost this amount in various unsuccessful business enterprises. She stated under oath that during the two years she had operated a cigar store in Dawson, she had made more than $60,000, and that she had brought that amount of cash with her when she left Dawson in 1900. Her story was that all the real estate holdings were hers.

In December 1923, the court concluded that all of the assets claimed by Marguerite were either the separate property of George Carmack or the community property of Marguerite and George Carmack.

The court ordered Marguerite to surrender all the

Carmack assets to Mr. Frye. After taking possession of the properties, he estimated their worth in excess of $150,000.

Marguerite appealed the decision of Judge Dykeman and the case went to the Supreme Court of the state of Washington. Graphie's lawyers contended that when Carmack made his strange will, it was clearly his intent that his daughter should receive half of his estate.

The prolonged litigation over the Carmack estate, with his wife and sister acrimoniously opposing each other in court, caused Jacob Saftig a great deal of agonizing concern. Jobless for months, he was broke. When Marguerite promised to give him $5,000 if he could induce Graphie to accept $5,000 as an out-of-court settlement in the estate lawsuits, he agreed to make the attempt. An angry Graphie indignantly refused the offer. She and her children moved out of their Berkeley apartment and moved in with Rose Curtis. A year later Graphie divorced her husband. Not only did Saftig lose his wife, but his failure to coerce her into accepting Marguerite's offer resulted in a lifetime estrangement between him and his sister.

Eventually, Marguerite instructed her attorneys to negotiate an out-of-court settlement with Graphie and her attorneys. An agreement was reached February 26, 1926, three years and eight months after the death of Carmack. In return for relinquishing all claims against the Carmack estate, Graphie received $45,000 cash, half of which went to her attorneys. Marguerite paid all the other legal fees, which were substantial. Administrator Herman Frye was paid $5,000 for his services, and his attorney received $10,000. Kate Carmack had died in 1920 and her estate received nothing; the attorney for her estate received $2,500. Marguerite had to mortgage her Seattle real estate to pay off all those involved in the settlement. Her equity in the Carmack estate was reduced to about $100,000.

Rose Curtis, who had loaned Graphie $1,000 so that she might prosecute her claim to a share of her father's estate, was not a beneficiary of the settlement. Rose and Frank Curtis quietly lived out the rest of their lives in Hollister. Rose, the first to go, died of pneumonia on March 29, 1938, at the age of 82.

After Graphie received her settlement, she married a used-car salesman named Couto with whom she went to Hollywood. From then on she always referred to herself as Grace, not Graphie. A year later she was broke. After a divorce from Couto, she married a sawmill worker and World War I veteran named Raymond Rogers. After he died, Graphie lived at Lodi, California, not far from the home of her daughter and grandchildren. In May 1960, when interviewed by the author, Graphie complained that her feet hurt and she wished she had a pair of Tagish-made moccasins. The author drew a contour of her feet on a sheet of paper and had a pair made for her when he returned to the Yukon. She died in 1963 at the age of 70.

After the estate was settled, Marguerite went back to California and continued to develop her gold mines. She visited Seattle every year to look after her properties there.

On October 11, 1929, while in Seattle, Marguerite made a handwritten will, a lengthy document consisting of eight sections dealing with the disposition of all her property, both real and personal. Still angry with her brother Jacob for failing to effect a settlement with Graphie, an unforgiving Marguerite cut him off with a bequest of five dollars. The remaining property she left to her sister and her niece in equal shares.

In 1933, Marguerite published George Carmack's discovery story in the form of an 18-page booklet called "My Experiences in the Yukon," with George W. Carmack shown as the author. Privately printed in Seattle, the booklet had only a limited distribution. Marguerite sent copies to the public libraries in Seattle, New York, Vancouver and elsewhere. Before publishing the booklet, Marguerite reviewed Carmack's manuscript, deleting all references to Kate and Graphie. She also went through Carmack's diaries and notebooks, cutting out pages dealing with his life with Kate.

Marguerite never lost faith in Carmack's Pacific Blue Lead and Snowshoe gold mines near Westville. For 18 years after her husband died, she spent considerable amounts of time, money and energy on the development of those placer operations. The deeper her workmen dug, the deeper Marguerite was obliged to dip into her dwindling resources. One by one she sold off her hotels and apartment houses in Seattle to raise money. By 1938 she owned nothing in Seattle but the house at 1522 East Jefferson Street where she and George had spent happy years together.

In 1941, Marguerite closed her mine and moved into the town of Auburn, in Placer County. For over a year she had been troubled by hypertension. On January 9, 1942, her physician, Dr. D.H. Kindopp, placed her in the Placer County Hospital at Auburn. She did not respond to treatment. At 10:50 A.M. on January 30, Marguerite Carmack, aged 68, suffered a fatal cerebral hemorrhage. Her body was cremated and the ashes buried beside her husband's grave in Seattle.

Marguerite's California estate consisted of three mining claims, one appraised at $500 and the other two at one dollar each, and her house in Seattle, appraised at $2,500. The house went to her niece, who repaid the $494 Marguerite had borrowed from her attorneys.

The fortune Marguerite had inherited from her husband had been taken out of the ground in the Klondike. She had poured most of the money back into the ground in California.

*   *   *

In 1892 George Carmack had established a trading post just above Five Finger Rapids at the confluence of the Big Salmon and Yukon rivers. The settlement that sprang up around the trading post grew into a town now known as Carmacks, on the Whitehorse-to-Dawson highway.

After the completion of the White Pass & Yukon railroad in 1900, the Chilkoot Pass trail fell into disuse, and the log bridges across the Taiya River eventually collapsed. As the thick underbrush grew up, sections of the trail disappeared. In the 1960s, the Canadian government and the new state of Alaska made a joint effort to restore that historic route to the Klondike. Crews were sent out to clear the brush, rebuild the bridges and construct overnight cabins for hikers. Every summer, several hundred men, women and children now make the 22-mile hike from Dyea to Lake Bennett. A few miles out of Dyea the Chilkoot Trail winds around the base of Mount Carmack, a magnificent 6,700-foot peak, crowned with seven glaciers, named by government surveyor John A. Fleming in 1898.

On the 79th anniversary of Discovery Day, August 17, 1975, the Alaska Yukon Pioneers of Seattle placed granite monuments on the graves of George and Marguerite Carmack in Seattle's Washelli Cemetery.

In 1926 the Alaska Yukon Pioneers, a Seattle organization, had commissioned sculptor Alonzo Victor Lewis to create a statue of heroic proportions to commemorate the intrepid sourdoughs who had participated in the gold rushes to Alaska and the Yukon. The organization planned to raise $25,000 so that a huge statue could be erected at a prominent location in downtown Seattle. They requested that Lewis fashion the statue in the likeness of the man who had started the Klondike Gold Rush, George Carmack, an early member of the organization. Because Carmack was dead, Lewis used photographs as a model to make a series of small clay statues. A mold made from one was used to cast a three-foot statue that the sculptor named "The Sour-dough."

Since 1981 this bronze statue of Carmack has been on display in the museum operated by the Klondike Gold Rush National Historical Park in Seattle's Pioneer Square. "The Sourdough" shows Carmack, a faraway look in his eyes, wearing his prospector's outfit, carrying a Model 94 Winchester in one hand and a stout walking stick in the other hand, and wearing a backpack that contains pan, pick and shovel.

George Carmack in Dawson City; the sketches were done by Art Buell, on Carmack's own copy of this photograph. (COURTESY ERNEST C. SAFTIG)

Sixty years after Carmack made his discovery, the Klondike River still runs swift and clear, blue-green in color under azure summer skies. In the willow groves at the mouth,
where Carmack once had his fish camp, bearded backpack-
ers now pitch their yellow nylon tents. Scavenging ravens
still prowl the mudflats at river's edge, their dismal croak-
ing mournful as ever.

Bonanza Creek, a shallow, gentle stream, continues to
meander through the rounded, birch-covered hills. Occasionally its clear waters are muddied by hilltop sluicers,
who in 1974 took more than 10,000 ounces of gold from the
Klondike. The claims once owned by George Carmack,
Skookum Jim and Tagish Charley now belong to the Canadian government. They are part of the Klondike Gold Rush
National Historical Park. A bronze plaque mounted on a
stone cairn marks the spot where George Carmack staked
his Discovery Claim.

A controversy over who should get credit for the discovery of gold on Bonanza continues to this day. There is no
question about who staked Discovery Claim: it was George
Carmack. Bob Henderson, however, claimed that he advised Carmack to prospect there. (The author remains convinced that Carmack's version is accurate.) The record
shows that Henderson had never set foot on Bonanza and
would have had little reason to advise Carmack to prospect
there.

Because Henderson had worked for William Redford on
Quartz Creek, which has its source near the top of the
Dome, he could have climbed to a vantage point on the
Dome to look around, and seen that three creeks originated
on the western slopes of the Dome. The most southerly one
was Quartz Creek. The northern one was Gold Bottom,
where Henderson later staked a claim. Between these two
was Rabbit Creek, which Carmack later renamed Bonanza

Creek. Henderson never got around to trying Rabbit Creek. Years later he was to claim that when he met Carmack at the mouth of the Klondike, he advised Carmack to try Rabbit Creek. Other records do not support Henderson's claim. Back in 1894, a year before Henderson went to work for him, William Redford was taking in more than $50 worth of gold a day from his Quartz Creek placer mine. Redford was the first man to sink a shaft to bedrock and the first man to operate a profitable mine in the Klondike region. Quartz Creek flows into the Indian River so it is not in the Klondike River watershed but since only narrow Dome Ridge separates the head of Quartz Creek from the head of Bonanza Creek, Quartz Creek is undeniably in the Klondike region.

Redford's Quartz Creek operation did not result in a great rush to the area, and Henderson's Gold Bottom claim, which he later abandoned, did not attract a swarm of prospectors. But George Carmack's discovery on Bonanza did trigger the big stampede to the Klondike.

The annual Discovery Day celebration in Dawson City, commemorating Carmack's August 17 strike on Bonanza Creek, is the big event of the year, with the customary parades and speeches. Traffic on the gravel streets kicks up a gray dust fine as baby powder that blankets the spruce planks of the sidewalks. Tourists clump along the narrow board walks, their footsteps making hollow plunking sounds. In the rebuilt Palace Grand Theatre, young women wearing Days of '98 costumes dance the can-can to the accompaniment of honky-tonk music. A few old-timers whose prospector friends or relatives knew Dawson when it was the richest, most exciting mining camp in North America relate to eager listeners the legendary tales of the olden, golden Klondike days, the days that are gone forever.

FOOTNOTES

CHAPTER 1
1. George Carmack, *My Experiences in the Yukon,* pp. 15–16.
2. *The Seattle Post-Intelligencer,* July 19, 1897.
3. *Ibid,* July 17, 1899.
4. *The Seattle Times,* July 16, 1922.

CHAPTER 2
1. Rose Watson, letter to George Carmack, February 27, 1887.
2. George Carmack, diary.

CHAPTER 3
1. George Carmack, letter to Rose Watson, August 18, 1885.
2. *Ibid.*

CHAPTER 4
1. George Carmack, letter to Rose Watson, November 10, 1885.
2. George Carmack, *My Experiences in the Yukon,* p. 7.

CHAPTER 5
1. George Carmack, *The Klondike News,* April 1, 1898.

CHAPTER 6
1. The narrative in this chapter is based on George Carmack's booklet, *My Experiences in the Yukon,* with additional information from author interviews with Graphie Carmack Rogers and Patsy Henderson.

CHAPTER 7
1. George Carmack, *My Experiences in the Yukon,* p. 13.

CHAPTER 8
1. Author interview with Graphie Carmack Rogers, May 28, 1960.
2. George Carmack, letter to Rose Watson, February 16, 1897.
3. Carmack, letter to Rose, June 20, 1897.

CHAPTER 9
1. Author interview with Ed Conrad.
2. *The Seattle Post-Intelligencer,* July 26, 1899.
3. *The Seattle Times,* July 27, 1899.
4. *The Seattle Post-Intelligencer,* July 27, 1899.
5. George Carmack, letter to Rose Watson, July 28, 1899.

CHAPTER 10
1. *In the Supreme Court of the State of Washington. In the Matter of the Estate of George Washington Carmack, Case Number 18829, Brief of Respondent,* pp. 14–15.
2. *Ibid.*
3. George Carmack, letter to Rose Watson, July 25, 1900.
4. Carmack, letter to Rose, August 18, 1900.

CHAPTER 11
1. George Carmack, letter to Rose Watson, October 15, 1900.
2. Carmack, letter to Rose, November 27, 1900.
3. Carmack, letter to Rose, November 13, 1900.
4. Carmack, letter to Rose, November 30, 1900.
5. Carmack, letter to Rose, December 12, 1900.
6. Carmack, letter to Rose, December 14, 1900.
7. Carmack, letter to Rose, January 19, 1901.

CHAPTER 12
1. Author interview with Mrs. Fred Boss, June 18, 1956.

CHAPTER 13
1. Author interview with Graphie Carmack Rogers, May 28, 1960.
2. *Ibid.*
3. George Carmack, letter to Rose Watson, August 1, 1907.
4. *The Seattle Post-Intelligencer,* May 30, 1909.
5. Carmack, letter to Rose, March 5, 1912.
6. Records of King County court.

CHAPTER 14
1. Marguerite Carmack, letter to George Carmack, November 21, 1917.
2. *The Vancouver Sun,* June 6, 1922.

ePILOGUE
1. Author interview with Graphie Carmack Rogers, May 28, 1960.

BIBLIOGRAPHY

BOOKS

Adney, Tappan. *The Klondike Stampede,* Harper & Brothers, New York, 1900.

Anonymous. *Memorial and Biographical History of the Coast Counties of Central California,* Lewis Publishing Co., 1893.

Bankson, Russel A. *The Klondike Nugget,* The Caxton Printers, Caldwell, Idaho, 1935.

Berton, Pierre. *The Klondike Fever,* Alfred A. Knopf, New York, 1958.

Cody, H. A. *Apostle of the North,* E. P. Dutton & Co., New York, 1913.

Curtain, Walter R. *Yukon Voyage,* The Caxton Printers, Caldwell, Idaho, 1938.

Kitchener, L. D. *Flag Over the North,* Superior Publishing Co., Seattle, 1954.

Ogilvie, William. *Early Days on the Yukon,* John Lane Co., New York, 1913.

Scidmore, E. R. *Alaska - Its Southern Coast and the Sitka Archipelago,* D. Lothrop and Co., Boston, 1885.

Shaw, George C. *The Chinook Jargon and How to Use it,* Rainier Printing Co., Seattle, 1909.

Sola, A. E. Ironmonger. *Klondike: Truth and Facts of the New Eldorado,* The Mining and Geographical Institute, London, 1897.

Wickersham, James. *Old Yukon: Tales - Trails - Trials,* The Washington Law Book Co., Washington, D.C., 1938.

NEWSPAPERS

The Alaska Weekly	Seattle, 1953.
The Dawson Daily News	Dawson, 1902.
The Dawson Weekly	Dawson, 1944.
The Dyea Trail	Dyea, 1898.
The Klondike News	San Francisco, 1898.
The Klondike Nugget	Dawson, 1898.
The San Francisco Call	San Francisco, 1897, 1900.
The San Francisco Chronicle	San Francisco, 1897, 1922, 1963.
The San Francisco Examiner	San Francisco, 1885, 1897.
The Seattle Post-Intelligencer	Seattle, 1897–1901, 1909, 1963.
The Seattle Times	Seattle, 1899, 1922, 1947.
The Sydney Morning Herald	Sydney, N.S.W., 1897.
The Vancouver Sun	Vancouver, B.C., 1922.
The Whitehorse Star	Whitehorse, Y.T., 1966, 1972.

GOVERNMENT DOCUMENTS

Klondike Mining District Records, Dawson, 1891–1901.

Klondike Official Guide, Department of Interior, Toronto, 1898.

Superior Court of King County, Seattle, case number 31527 & 61532.

Superior Court of Placer County, Auburn, case number 5543.
Supreme Court of the State of Washington, Olympia, case 18829.
U. S. Marine Corps Records, National Archives, Washington, 1881, 1882.
U. S. S. *Pinta* deck log, National Archives, Washington, 1885.
U. S. S. *Wachusett* deck log, National Archives, Washington, 1881, 1882.

PERIODICALS

Alaska Yukon Magazine, 1908, 1920.
Alaska Sportsman, 1968.
The Australian Mining Record, 1897.
The Pathfinder, published by the Pioneers of Alaska, 1920, 1921.

UNPUBLISHED SOURCES

Alaska Yukon Pioneers, Seattle, biographical files.
Carmack, George, letters to Rose Watson, 1883–1922.
Griffith, David E., unfinished manuscript on mining in the Yukon found in the
    files of the Alaska Yukon Pioneers, Seattle. Portions of the manuscript were
    published in *The Seattle Times* in 1947.
Phillips Letter Collection, Yukon Archives, Whitehorse.
Yukon Order of Pioneers, Lodge number 2, Seattle, biographical files.

INDEX